I'm Not Weird

I'm Just Quiet!

J.F. WIEGAND

Visit the author's website at www.jfwiegand.com

CONTENTS

1) Survival Skills

2) The House Guest

3) The Bet

4) Fire Drill

5) Practice

6) Taco Tuesday

7) The Brick Wall

8) The Debate

9)The Recovery

CHAPTER 1

SURVIVAL SKILLS

I know what's coming. It's the same three words that have been used to describe me two-hundred and seventy-eight times over the first twelve years of my life.

This chatty redhead who sits next to me will have the honor of delivering these words for the two-hundred and seventy-ninth time. She's describing each of her classmates' personalities to a new girl who's starting in our class today.

She points to the boy sitting in front of me. "That's Ronald Winkler. He has bad breath and wears the same shirt every day. I'd stay away from him."

Then her eyes shift to me. "That's Colin Quigley."

Here it comes. Number two-hundred and seventy-nine.

"He's really quiet."

And she says it like I have a disease, as if I was born with this hopeless medical condition. I can picture the doctor handing me to my parents. "Sorry, Mr. and Mrs. Quigley, he's quiet."

I already know I'm quiet, so I'm not sure why people have to remind me every couple of days.

As I watch the new girl's reaction, I'm surprised to see a smile spread across her face. I was certain that she would pile on, but she's smiling as if she understands what I'm going through. Maybe she's quiet too. It'd be nice to add another member to the team. That would make three in my class: Ronald, the new girl, and me.

Another person who understands is my teacher, Ms. Walsh. Although Ms. Walsh has to talk a lot during class, I'm pretty sure she's quiet too. Whenever I see her in the teachers' lounge, she's sitting by herself reading a book.

Ms. Walsh knows I'm quiet, so she treats me differently than the other students. She never calls on me unless I raise my hand, she avoids asking me questions that require more than a one-word response, and she finds ways to give me time to myself.

After taking attendance, Ms. Walsh scans the class over the rim of her glasses. Her eyes lock with mine. "Colin, can you take the attendance sheet down to the office?"

Yes! Three minutes alone!

She's supposed to let the students take turns bringing down the attendance sheet, but I go at least once a week.

On my way to the office, I see Principle Reiland farther down the hall, his dress shoes clicking against the floor as he walks. I slow down so he doesn't see me. If he sees me, he'll want to talk, and I'll have enough talking to do during lunch so I need to conserve my energy.

Just to be sure he doesn't spot me, I kneel down and pretend to tie my shoe. It's not actually untied, so I have to untie it first and then retie it. I do the same thing with my other shoe. After he disappears around the corner, I continue to the office.

Most of my day is made up of these little encounters, or lack of encounters. They're crucial to my survival because talking is exhausting. I think it's that way for all quiet kids.

My talk-capacity, as I like to call it, is three-hundred and thirteen words. Once I reach that limit, I get frustrated, grumpy, and eventually shut down. And the only thing that can restore my talk capacity is time to myself. So whenever I have an opportunity for alone time, even if it's just a minute, I take it. That way, when I do have to talk, I have enough energy to get the words out.

***

I eat lunch with Perry Miller and Nate Dabrowski, my two best friends at John Quincy Adams Middle School. We're all in the seventh grade, but this year we're only in a couple of classes together. They're quiet like me, which is why I'm friends with them. I don't have any close friends who aren't quiet. It just wouldn't work.

We sit at a table in the corner of the cafeteria, as far away from the talkative crowd as possible. I've noticed that the chattier someone is, the more likely they are to sit in the middle of a room. So the closer we can sit to a wall, the less chance we have of being sucked into a conversation.

"Have you seen the new janitor?" Perry asks, joining me at our usual table. "That dude's an alien."

Perry's not kidding when he says that. He's obsessed with aliens. He's convinced that all of the cleaning and cafeteria workers are from another planet.

What's funny, though, of all the people I know, Perry looks the most like an alien. He's tall and lanky, with hollow eyes and long fingers.

Nate drops his lunch down, giving us a weak wave. He sits down next to Perry, lets out a yawn, and looks over at me with droopy eyes.

"What are the odds that you fall asleep today?" I ask.

"Do you want it as odds-for, odds-against, or a percentage?" he asks.

"Percentage."

"Ninety-one," Nate says. "He talked until 12:06 AM."

Nate has a twin named Dexter, who is one of the nicest guys in school, but also talks an awful lot, which doesn't work well with Nate's personality. Plus, they share a room, so it's hard for Nate to get any time to himself.

Glancing over my shoulder, I see Dexter sitting at his usual table in the middle of the cafeteria. Dexter and Nate aren't identical twins, but it's still hard to tell they're brothers. Aside from their pale skin, they look and sound completely different. Dexter is animated and his face bright, whereas Nate talks in a monotone voice and rarely smiles.

I don't think I'd do well with a twin. I could handle the matching outfits, but the constant interaction would exhaust me, especially if we had to share a room.

Then we all begin to eat. We have an unspoken rule about keeping our conversations short. I love unspoken rules.

"Can I join you?" a girl asks.

I look up and see the new student from my class. I think her name is Sophia.

Perry and I glance at each other and then back to her. She sits down before we can answer, and my loud-girl radar immediately goes off. I can already tell Sophia's impatient, a good indication she's a talker.

"So you believe in UFOs?" Sophia asks Perry.

He taps his alien-like fingers against the table. "That sure seems like an odd question."

"Not really," Sophia says. "Your shirt has a picture of a UFO on it ... and underneath it says *I believe.*"

Perry shrugs.

"You know, if you're interested in UFOs," Sophia says, "you should read *The Earthling from* —"

"*Outer Space*, yes, I've read it," Perry says.

Sophia smiles. "A fellow science fiction reader ..."

I'm a science fiction reader too, but there's no way I'll tell her. If I tell her, she'll just want to talk about it.

"You should read *The Sixth Galaxy,*" she says to Perry.

Perry sighs. "Yes, yes, I've read it. And I've read the sequels too, *The Seventh Galaxy* and *The Eighth Galaxy.*"

"I hear there's going to be a fourth," she says. "Fourth book I mean, not fourth galaxy."

Perry rubs his eyes and exhales. His energy level is fading. I need to step in and save him, otherwise things could get ugly.

"You know, you might want to try that table," I say to her, motioning to a group of loud kids who are blabbering away at another table.

Nate rubs his eyes. "That's an excellent idea."

"Why?" she asks.

"We just think you might, you know, have more in common with them," I say. "Those kids are a little more talkative."

"No, I'm good here," she says, and then studies my face. "You're Colin, right?"

I nod. I like questions that don't require a verbal response.

"So how do you like Ms. Walsh?" she asks.

Now this type of question I'm not crazy about. It's open-ended, the worst kind of question for quiet people. I keep my response short, hoping the lack of detail will discourage additional questions. "She's good."

"What do you like about her?"

Okay, so that didn't work out so well, and after six more open-ended questions I'm spent. Sophia seems nice, but she talks *way* too much. It's time I ended our conversation.

"I'm going to class," I say, shoving the rest of my salami sandwich into my mouth.

"Really?" Sophia asks. "What time is it?"

I raise my forearm and rotate it so my watch is facing her. This saves me the few words it takes to say the time.

"It's only quarter after twelve," she says, squinting at my watch. "Lunch isn't over for another fifteen minutes."

I swallow the last bite, pulling my arm back. "I know, but I forgot to do my history homework."

This isn't true, and I feel bad for lying, but it's the only way. I need that time to myself to recharge.

As I begin to walk away, I hear Nate snoring.

***

8

My goal on the bus is to sit by myself.

As I board the bus in the afternoon, I begin scanning the rows for empty seats, starting with the back. Most kids sit toward the front, so the back of the bus tends to be less crowded. But I don't sit all the way in the back because that's where the troublemakers sit. They tend to take up the last few rows. So I try to target the third or fourth row from the back, This gives me the best chance of sitting alone.

And just to be safe, I pick a seat that's in bad shape. I've been riding bus 310 since the fall and there's a seat four rows from the back, along the right side, that has a bad tear in it. The tear keeps kids away.

Larry and Stanley Botchaway, two brothers who live next to me, stroll down the aisle. I position myself in the middle of my seat and glance out the window. The lack of available seat space deters other riders from sitting next to me. I also never look anyone in the eye because that's an automatic invitation to sit down.

The Botchaway brothers pass my seat and continue to the back of the bus. Now, I do consider Larry and Stanley troublemakers, so they may have sat in the back regardless, but still, I've had a seat to myself for forty-seven straight days. I must be doing something right.

Using these strategies throughout the day allows me to have a sufficient talk-capacity at home. It's here, at four Queen Street in northern Virginia, where *I* am the talker.

But it's only possible because being quiet runs in my family. I just happen to be the loudest of the bunch. My father is quiet, his father was quiet, and his father's father was quiet. I'm sure it goes on and on after that. Naturally my father married a quiet woman. My mother tends to be a little more talkative than my father, but just barely. And when a quiet father and a quiet mother have children, those children are *always* quiet. My sister Violet is fifteen, three years older than me, but she's much quieter. In fact, it's been an entire week since I've heard her speak.

Violet looks a lot like me. We both have light brown hair, brown eyes, and we're a little on the short side. I guess the only difference, aside from her being a girl, is that her hair is longer. In fact, Violet's hair is halfway down her back. She says she's growing it out, but I think she's afraid of getting it cut because that would require a conversation with a hairdresser. I'm certain she wants no part of that.

Tonight is Friday and that means we're having pizza. My family is one of habit and every Friday is pizza night. It's our usual order: one medium cheese and one medium pepperoni. We Quigleys don't get too crazy with our toppings.

It's my night to set the table. I go every Tuesday and Friday. On each placemat, I add a plate, napkin, fork, knife, and spoon. The napkin goes on the left side with the fork on top of it, and the knife and spoon go on the right. We probably won't need utensils for the pizza, but I like to be consistent. We also have assigned seats. My mom and dad sit at the heads of the table, and Violet and I sit on each side, with my seat facing the window. It's a nice view into the back yard.

"Let's eat," my father says. It's usually the only thing he says during dinner.

I bite into my first slice and then get the dinner conversation rolling. "I got an A on my math test."

My mother's face brightens. "An A? That's terrific."

"I also came in second during the mile run in gym," I say. "I finished in seven minutes and nine seconds."

"That's fast," my mother says.

"And during music class, I—"

Violet clenches her fists and huffs.

My mother doesn't have to ask her what's wrong. She already knows. Violet wants me to stop talking so she can eat her pizza in silence.

"Colin's just telling us about his day, honey. You know, you should try being more talkative like your brother."

Violet shakes her head and her long hair snaps in the air, whipping back and forth.

"Okay, Violet," my mother says, holding up her hands. "You can go eat in the—"

Violet is in the family room before my mother can finish her sentence.

I like Violet, mostly because I can relate to her. I understand what she's going through, so I try to limit my talking when she's around. I like my mom and dad too, and the good thing about having quiet parents is that they rarely embarrass me in front of my friends. Embarrassing me involves talking, and that doesn't happen too often with my folks.

That night in bed, just before I fall asleep, one final thought drifts through my head. *I have a nice, quiet life.*

CHAPTER 2

THE HOUSE GUEST

A strange sound awakens me on Saturday morning, one that I don't hear very often downstairs. It sounds like ... talking, and not just a few exchanges. There's serious babbling going on down there and lots of it.

I get dressed and head down. The chatter is getting louder as I approach the kitchen. It's a girl's voice, one I'm not familiar with. Whoever she is, she talks loud, *real* loud. I enter the kitchen and discover the source of this annoying, squeaky voice. The girl, probably my age, has short, spiky black hair and a gigantic mouth. And I'm not saying that because she talks a lot. Her mouth is literally gigantic, like she could fit a grapefruit into it.

"Colin," my mother says, "this is your cousin Reagan. Do you remember her? I know it's been awhile."

Reagan's a lot bigger than I remember. She's about three inches taller than me, and her arms and legs are about twice the size of mine. She's the daughter of my Uncle Tom and I think she lives in Texas. I hear that everything is bigger in Texas. I guess that goes for people's mouths too. My Uncle Tom is even quieter than my mom so I'm shocked that Reagan is so talkative.

"There's no way he remembers me," Reagan says. "I look different now."

Yeah, your mouth has exploded since I last saw you, is what I'm thinking, but I try to be polite. "No, I remember you."

"The only thing I remember about you," Reagan says, "is that you were like crazy-quiet."

Make that two-hundred and eighty.

It wasn't the usual three words, but I still count it. I accept several variations. I'll be honest too, I'm not sure it's exactly two-hundred and eighty. I think it's pretty close though. The exact number since I started counting at age six is one-hundred and thirty-eight, which works out to twenty-three a year over six years. So I did the math: twenty-three times twelve equals two-hundred and seventy-six, and I've had four more since my twelfth birthday. A grand total of two-hundred and eighty.

I think about how pointless Reagan's statement is. If I'm quiet, and she calls me quiet, what have we really accomplished?

"I didn't offend you, did I?" Reagan asks. "I know some kids don't like being called quiet."

I raise my shoulders. "I don't care."

"Colin's quite chatty now," my mom says.

Reagan shakes her head and snickers. "I'll believe it when I hear it."

"Did your father tell you?" my mom asks me. "Reagan's going to be staying with us for a few weeks."

My mouth drops open. "What? Why?"

"Uncle Tom received a job offer in Virginia. They're going to be moving here."

"It doesn't sound like a good job if he can't afford his own house."

"No, silly, they're getting their own house. They just wanted Reagan to get started with school while they sell their place in Texas. Isn't it great that your cousin's going to be staying with us?"

What's the opposite of great?

"So how many kids are in your school?" Reagan asks as she shoves a wad of bubblegum into her mouth.

I rub my eyes, still trying to wake up. "Uh ... I ... I don't know."

"How many kids are in your class?" Reagan asks.

"Do you mean like the entire seventh grade or ... just my class?"

"The entire seventh grade."

"I'm not sure."

She blows a bubble and continues talking. "What about your class?"

I peek around the bubble as it expands in front of her face. "I think there's twenty-one."

"Does that include the teacher?"

"No. Why would it ..." I stop myself, too tired to finish the question.

The bubble pops. She peels it from her face and slides the gum back into her mouth. "Do you have stadium seating in your classrooms?"

"Stadium seating? Like a movie theatre?"

"Yeah. That's what we have at my school in Texas." She shifts her legs and puts a hand on her hip. "Texas is big and so are the schools."

"No, we don't have stadium seating. They're just regular classrooms."

16

"So what does your school serve for lunch?"

The questions just keep coming. I can't keep up. She's already worn me out and I haven't even had breakfast.

"It depends which day," I say.

"What about Monday?"

I close my eyes, trying to recall the schedule. My brain is starting to hurt. "I think ... I don't know ... I'd have to look at the lunch calendar."

"You're not a morning person are you, Colin?"

If she's going to insult me, I wish she could at least do it with a statement and not another question. It's bad enough, but now I have to respond.

The weekend goes downhill from there. Although the questions gradually slow, the talking doesn't. I spend the rest of the day listening to Reagan talk about her dog, her trampoline, her shoe size, her favorite shirt, her favorite pants, her favorite TV show, her favorite lumberjack—that's right, lumberjack—her dessert preferences, her juggling skills, sugar cereals, waffles, grits, an explanation on the different types of eggs, how much she can bench press, how much she can curl, the danger of swallowing gum, football, hockey, horseshoes, the Battle of the Alamo, the difference between affect and effect, witches, ghosts, vampires, and why it's bad to look directly at the sun.

And that's just what made it through. My brain rejected everything after that point because I had reached my listening-capacity limit. My listening-capacity is much higher than my talk-capacity, but she still managed to deplete it in a matter of minutes.

***

I step softly down the stairs on Sunday morning. Since we only have three bedrooms, Reagan is sleeping on the couch and the last thing I want to do is wake the talking-giant.

I was a little surprised that my parents made Reagan sleep on the couch, but what option did they have? They know that to Violet and me, our bedrooms are everything. They're where we go to reenergize. Without our bedrooms we'd be walking zombies, unable to function in society.

I step through the kitchen like a fawn pattering by a sleeping lion. Reagan is snoring and it sounds like someone playing the trumpet, but badly. I quietly fill a bowl with my favorite cereal, Rice Krispies, but as soon as I pour the milk and my cereal starts to pop, the beast awakens.

"Is that Rice Krispies?" Reagan says, springing off the couch.

I should have gone with Cheerios.

She plops down at the table, her large mouth salivating. "I'm starving. Pour me a bowl too."

I sigh and grab another bowl.

"No, no, no," she says. "I like to use big bowls for my cereal. You know, like a bowl you would mix something in."

"I don't know where we keep those bowls," I say.

Her eyes scan the kitchen. "What about a pot? Do you have any big pots?"

I search the cabinets until I find our biggest pot. I think my mom uses it to make spaghetti. I fill the pot with Rice Krispies, pour half a jug of milk over it, and then grab a spoon.

"That's too small," Reagan says. "I want a bigger spoon, like a serving spoon."

"What's a serving spoon?"

"It's one of those spoons you serve macaroni and cheese with."

I find an oversized spoon and jam it into the gigantic pan of Rice Krispies. Reagan licks her lips and her eyes widen. She slides the pot in front of her, shoves a massive spoonful of Rice Krispies into her mouth, and begins jabbering away.

"I think they should add a fourth Rice Krispies character," she says, looking at the front of the cereal box.

I sit down across from her. "I like the three they have."

"No, they need to add a fourth. They could call him *Bam*."

"Bam?"

"Yeah, you know, snap, crackle, pop, and BAM!" As she says it, four Rice Krispies fly out of her mouth and onto my shirt.

I brush them off. "But Rice Krispies don't go snap, crackle, pop, and ... bam. It's just snap, crackle, and pop."

"That's what I'm saying, they should change it. They should make them go snap, crackle, pop, and BAM!" she says, slamming her fist against the table.

"But they'd have to change how the cereal sounds when you pour the milk on. How would they do that?"

"I don't know, they could figure it out. They were able to make it go snap, crackle, and pop, so I'm sure they could change it to go snap, crackle, pop, and BAM!" Both her hands pound against the table. "Or you know what, maybe it should be snap, crackle, pop, and BOOM! Wait, no, they should alternate it. First it would be snap, crackle, pop, and BAM! Then it would be snap, crackle, pop, and BOOM! BAM! BOOM! BAM! BOOM!"

After the final *boom*, I'm certain the entire house is awake.

A moment later, Violet walks into the kitchen. She sees Reagan and stops, her eyes bulging open. Holding her breath, Violet steps backwards until she's out of the kitchen, and then turns and hurries back up the stairs. My sister would rather starve than be in the same room with Reagan.

***

When I board the bus on Monday morning, I'm exhausted. I'm normally at one-hundred percent talk-capacity on Mondays because I've had extra quiet time over the weekend, but not today, not even close. I'll be lucky just to get a few words out.

Reagan follows me onto the bus. This will be her first day at John Quincy Adams Middle School. I take my usual seat, the one with the rip, but Reagan doesn't notice and scoots in next to me. My streak of forty-seven straight days of sitting by myself has ended.

Reagan comments on how small the bus is and proceeds to talk for six and a half minutes about the school buses in Texas. Then she goes on an eleven minute rant about her old gym teacher, Ms. Hammerfield, who apparently can bench press four-hundred pounds, slam dunk a basketball, and kick eighty yard field goals. Who knew gym teachers in Texas were so amazing?

I barely process any of it. I just stare out the window wondering how this girl could possibly be related to me.

***

In first period, Ms. Walsh hands me a hall pass and tells me to get a drink of water. She must have noticed the dark circles under my eyes and wanted to give me some relief. Ms. Walsh sure knows a tired, quiet kid when she sees one.

At lunchtime, I'm the first one out of my class. I power-walk down the hall and make it to the cafeteria before anyone else. Arriving early, and the fact that I packed my lunch, should provide me with valuable alone time. By my estimation, I should have approximately four minutes before anyone arrives at my table, and I need it too. Although I was quieter than usual during my first few classes, I'm still functioning well below my talk-capacity due to the last few days with Reagan. But before I can take a bite of my sandwich, Sophia arrives. She has also packed her lunch. I wasn't counting on that.

"Hi, Colin," she says, her face bright and smiling. "The lunch-packers always reach the table first."

"I've never noticed that," I say, then look away, hoping to avoid a conversation.

"What are you having for lunch?" she asks.

I'm going to have to work on my looking away skills. They're not as effective as they once were. I turn back to Sophia, and as I do, I notice a striking resemblance between her and my mother. She's like a younger version of her, just a hundred times more talkative.

"Just a sandwich," I say.

She leans forward and looks at my sandwich. "Chicken?"

"Turkey."

"Close," she says, still smiling. "What are your sides?"

I show her my pretzels, apple slices, and grape juice.

"Check it out," she says, and whips outs potato chips, grapes, and cranberry juice.

This is unusual behavior for someone so talkative. It's normally just us quiet kids who have such organized, well balanced lunches. Loud kids are much more spontaneous with their food choices. In fact, last month this loud kid brought a jar of pickles to the cafeteria. That was it, just one jar of pickles. That was his entire lunch.

Perry and Nate finally arrive. Nate sits between Sophia and me, blocking the line of communication. I'll have to thank him for that later. Perry looks weary, like he hasn't slept in days. I'm used to seeing Nate like this, but not Perry.

"What's wrong?" I ask him.

"There's this new girl that started today ... she's been in all of my classes," Perry says with a whimper. "And twice they put her right next to me ..." He takes a few deep breaths, trying to gather the energy to continue. "She doesn't stop talking. She's like a jackhammer. Rat-tat-tat-tat ..."

His head drops to the table with a loud thud.

"Does she have spiky hair and a mouth the size of a large pizza?" I ask Perry.

"Yeah ... it's the biggest mouth I've ever seen." He lifts his head. "Do you know her?"

"She's my cousin."

"That's impossible. She can't be related to you."

"I know. I think she might be adopted."

A tray slams on the table. "Perry!" Reagan's voice echoes through the cafeteria. "You know Colin? Awesome. We can all eat together."

Perry's head crashes back down.

"Perry, you don't look so good," says Reagan, sitting next to me.

"He doesn't feel well," I say.

"What's wrong with him?" she says.

"It's complicated."

Reagan tosses a tater tot into her mouth. "Oh well."

I can feel Reagan's huge leg rubbing against mine, and every time she sucks down a tater tot, her elbow hits my arm. The table seems so small now.

Reagan notices Nate. "Who are you?"

Nate looks over at her with a straight, tired face. "Nate."

"Who is this dude, Colin? He seems weird."

"He's not weird. He my friend."

Reagan shakes her head at him. "Well he doesn't look good. I think he caught whatever disease Perry has."

Nothing that a little alone time couldn't cure.

Reagan's elbow bangs against my arm again as she hurls three more tater tots into her mouth.

"So what do you want to do after school, Colin?" she asks. "I was thinking of organizing a neighborhood football game. What do you think? Do you play football?"

"I've only played once. It was with Perry in my backyard and he broke his arm on the first play."

"You should play. You could be my kicker."

"Your kicker?"

"Yeah, I need a field goal kicker, and you kind of remind me of a kicker. They're quiet and a little weird."

Technically she didn't call *me* quiet, so I decide not to count this as number two-hundred and eighty-one. Although I am annoyed that she threw in the word 'weird.'

"How do you know kickers are quiet?" I ask.

"Because they never talk to anyone. They just wander around on the sidelines by themselves." Reagan scans the table for potential players, and then looks back to me. "Do you have good hang time on your kicks? I need a punter too. They're not as quiet as you, but they do tend to be loners."

Okay, I'm counting that one. That's two-hundred and eighty-one.

As Reagan starts gabbing again, this time about starting a school arm-wrestling team, I realize I'm in deep trouble. If I have to spend my entire lunch talking to her, I'll be wiped out.

Wait, I know.

"Hey Reagan, do you know Sophia?"

They talk for the next twenty-four glorious minutes. I'm able to make it through the rest of lunch with only saying eleven more words.

***

I come into the kitchen that night, my eyes heavy. Even with my quick thinking at lunch, Reagan has depleted most of my energy. Then I find her sitting in my seat at the dinner table. I stand there, pointing, my mouth open.

"Are you okay, Colin?" my mother asks.

Reagan turns and looks at me. "Why are you pointing at me?"

My arm stays outstretched, my eyes locked on the chair. "I'm pointing at the chair."

"Why are you pointing at the chair?" Reagan asks.

"Because it's my ..."

"You're over here tonight, honey," my mother says, waiving me to the other side of the table. Violet is sitting at the corner, cowering by my mother's side.

I lower my arm. "But ..."

"We got the office chair for you," my father says, rolling it out from underneath the table. "Genuine leather."

I sigh, and then walk around the table, my feet dragging. I sink into the chair, which sits much lower than my usual seat. My head barely clears the table. I reach under the chair and pull the lever, attempting to raise it.

"It's not moving."

"Yeah, sorry," my dad says. "The lever's broken."

My shoulders sag. "You said it was genuine leather."

Reagan shakes her head. "The leather doesn't make the chair go up and down, Colin."

I stare over at her. She has her knife and fork gripped tightly in each hand as if she's going to attack the spaghetti rather than eat it. I look down at my plate and utensils. I'm missing a napkin, and my fork and knife are both on the right side.

"This isn't right," I say.

"What?" my mother asks.

"The place setting. It's all messed up." I move the fork to the left of my plate, then notice something else. "And where's the spoon?"

"Why do you need a spoon for spaghetti?" asks Reagan.

"That's not the point," I say. "Each place setting should have a knife, fork *and* spoon."

"It was Reagan's first time," my mother says. "And she's right, we probably won't need the spoon."

I lift up my plate, looking underneath. "But there's no napkin either."

Reagan props her elbows on the table, the knife and fork still in her hands. "They're in the middle of the table, where they belong."

I shake my head, grab a napkin, and then place it under my fork.

"Okay," my dad says. "Let's eat."

Reagan devours her plate of spaghetti before I can even take my first bite. Then she grabs four pieces of garlic bread. My mom made eight, which normally works out to two a person. That's assuming there are four people, but tonight we have a guest, and that guest ate four pieces herself, leaving only one each for the rest of us.

"How was your first day of school?" my mother asks Reagan.

"I made like a hundred friends, organized a weekly football game, started an arm-wresting club, and joined the debate team."

My mother's eyes widen. "That's some first day."

"I've had better," says Reagan, raising her shoulders.

"So what else do you like to do, Reagan?" my mother asks. "I think Violet was still into princesses at your age."

"I'm not crazy about princesses, Mrs. Q. The ones in the books are kind of wimpy if you ask me." Reagan licks spaghetti sauce from the side of her mouth and continues. "But if I did have to pick one, I'd choose Jasmine because she's the richest and has the biggest palace. And palaces are great places to hear echoes. I love hearing my voice echo." She leans forward in her seat, excited. "ECHOOOOO!"

Reagan listens for the echo. "I didn't hear it. I think your house is too small. I can hear it when I do it at my house in Texas."

She shoves a piece of garlic bread into her mouth and keeps talking as she chews. "I wouldn't pick Aladdin as my boyfriend though. He's way too quiet. And his three wishes were terrible. If I were Aladdin, my first wish would have been to get rid of that annoying monkey, my second wish would have been to get a better monkey, and my third wish would have been to get a million dollars." She finishes the rest of her garlic bread and keeps talking. "I guess Ariel would be okay. It would be cool to swim through the ocean like she does. I'd swallow tons of crabs and lobsters."

The image of Reagan as a fish goes through my head. I envision her as a Big Mouth Bass.

She points across the table. "Can you pass the spaghetti, Mrs. Q?"

"Reagan, you can call me Aunt," my mother says.

"I can't, Mrs. Q. I get the willies when I say the word Aunt. It reminds me of ants, you know, like the bugs. I also don't like saying Uncle. Sorry, Mr. Q."

"What's wrong with using Uncle?" my mother asks. "What does that remind you of?"

"It still reminds me of ants. Not because Uncle sounds like ants, but because aunts and uncles are kind of like the same thing, so saying uncle reminds me of aunts, which reminds me of ants."

"Okay ..." my mother says, raising an eyebrow. She passes Reagan the bowl of spaghetti and then turns to me. "You've been quiet tonight, Colin."

That makes two-hundred and eighty-two. And from my mother no less!

I shrug, unable to even open my mouth.

"I think Reagan has moved ahead of you as the talker in the house," my mother says.

As Reagan fills her plate with more food, she peers over at me and grins. I don't have the energy to fight back.

It's official. My reign as house-talker has ended.

CHAPTER 3
THE BET

I lie in bed the next morning staring up at the ceiling. Although I slept for thirteen hours, I can't stop yawning, and it doesn't take me long to figure out why. The answer is sleeping on the couch downstairs.

And if this is my condition after a few days with her, I can't imagine how I'm going to feel in two weeks. I wonder if there's medicine I could take, something that would make me immune to loud people.

Through half-open eyes, I spot my mom walking by my room. I throw off the covers and hurry toward the door.

"Mom," I whisper, waving her inside.

"What is it, Colin?" she asks, stepping into my room. "Why are you being so quiet?"

I ease the door closed. "I didn't want to wake Reagan."

"Well that's considerate of you."

As I open my mouth to respond, I hear my alarm clock go off, blasting a high-pitched beeping through the room. I gasp, dart toward my nightstand, and dive, slamming my hand on the snooze-button.

"Colin, what are you—"

"Shhh!" I listen for movement downstairs. It's quiet.

I let out a slow breath, get up, and then drag my mom to the corner of my room, as far away from the door as possible. I am still trying to be considerate after all.

"What is going on?" she asks. "Is everything okay?"

I keep my voice low. "Yeah, yeah, I just wanted to talk to you about something."

"Sure. What?"

I look down and fiddle with my fingers. "It's about Reagan."

"Okay." she says, crossing her arms. "What about her?"

"How long do you think she'll be here for?"

"Just until her parents sell their house."

"Do you think they'll sell it today?"

"I doubt it. It will be at least a month."

34

I swallow hard and look up. "Why does it take so long to sell a house? I sold my old bike in like an hour."

"It's a little more complicated with a house."

"But couldn't they give like a prize to the person who buys it?"

She scratches her head, tilting it to the side. "A prize?"

"Yeah, that's what I did with my bike. I offered Timmy Nugent a Kit Kat and that sealed it."

"Well, I'll certainly give Uncle Tom your suggestion, but if no one goes for the Kit Kat, it could be a few months. Maybe even a year."

My eyes open wide. "*A year.*"

"Possibly. Why? Is there a problem with Reagan?"

"Well, she doesn't ... seem to fit in with us."

"Maybe not so much with Violet, but I thought the two of you would be up every night gabbing away."

I'd rather be eaten by a lion.

I shake my head. "I don't think we're going to have too many gab sessions, Mom."

"Okay, okay." She unfolds her arms and clasps her hands together. "What can I do to make it better?"

"Could Reagan stay in the backyard, like in a tent?"

My mom stares at me. "I'm not going to make Reagan sleep in the backyard."

"Could we put her in the basement?"

"She's not a dog, Colin."

"What if she got her own apartment, like in the city?"

"*No*. She's twelve." My mom puts her arm around me and pats me on my shoulder. "I know she can be a little overbearing, but give her a chance, okay. I think you'll grow to like her."

My mom crosses to the door. "I'm going down for breakfast. Do you want me to pour you a bowl of Rice Krispies?"

"No! No Rice Krispies!"

***

History is my only class with Reagan. Although she sits three desks away, it doesn't stop her from talking to me.

"Colin," she says, as class is about to begin.

I peek around the students between us.

She presses two of her fingers together as if she's pretending to hold something. "I need a pencil."

I keep three extra pencils in the front pocket of my backpack, so I guess I can spare one. I'll just have to remember to replace it as soon as I get home. I pull out one of the pencils and hand it to the girl sitting next to me, who then hands it to Ronald Winkler, who's sitting

36

next to her. Ronald stares at it. He's wearing his usual brown shirt and based on the look on Reagan's face, I think his breath still stinks.

"Can you pass it to Reagan?" I ask Ronald.

Before he can do anything, Reagan snatches the pencil from his hand.

"Thanks weirdo," she says. "And buy yourself a Tic Tac, would you?"

Ronald's face goes red. I wish Reagan would keep her opinions to herself. Not only is her comment rude, it's also inaccurate. I don't think you can buy Tic Tacs individually.

As Mr. Melacki begins his lecture, Reagan calls to me again. "Colin."

I sigh, then mouth the word 'what' to her.

"I need paper too," she says.

What does she carry in her backpack? Just tater tots?

I flip open my notebook, tear out a piece of paper, and then hand it to the girl next to me, who hands it to Ronald. He holds the sheet out in front of him with two shaking hands. Reagan yanks it from him.

"Colin," she says.

I sit there, looking straight ahead, pretending not to hear her this time.

"Colin," she says again. "I need a pencil with a better eraser."

I don't answer.

"*Colin.*"

Ten minutes later, my head is pounding, but this time it's not from Reagan, who ended up taking Ronald's pencil. It's from Mr. Melacki. He's going on and on about the Boston Tea Party. His entire summary of the event could have been accomplished in one simple sentence: A bunch of angry colonists threw tea into the harbor because the British government was being mean.   See, was that so hard?

Mr. Melacki then asks, "Does anyone know when this happened? When this iconic event in American history took place? When this turning point was in the colonists' resistance?"

He's already mentioned the date six or seven times, but I guess he forgot. I also don't know why he has to ask the same question three different ways. I raise my hand, hoping a direct answer will put him back on track.

He stares at me. "Uh ... Cameron?"

Quiet kids don't raise their hands that often, and because of it, teachers have trouble remembering our names. But they never have trouble remembering the loud kids' names, and why would they? The loud kids are always being told to be quiet.

"It's Colin," I say.

"You're too quiet, Colin, that's the problem. Why don't we make a deal ... you stop being so quiet and I'll start remembering your name."

Okay, I'll go ahead and count that as two: two-hundred and eighty-three and two-hundred and eighty-four. Oh, and no deal Mr. Melacki.

"Is it December sixteenth, 1773?" I ask.

"It is," he says. "You're a bright kid, Connor. You should speak up more."

I don't bother correcting him this time. He's just going to forget it again.

"So who can tell me the names of the three ships involved in the Boston Tea Party?" Mr. Melacki asks.

No hands go up.

"I'll give you a hint," he says. "One of the ships was named after an animal."

"Tiger!" says Reagan.

"Nope," Mr. Melacki says.

"Giraffe!" says Reagan.

Mr. Melacki shakes his head.

"Zebra!!" Reagan's voice is rising with each guess, as if her chances will improve the louder she shouts.

"Not a Zebra, "Mr. Melacki says.

This is ridiculous. There must be like ten-thousand different animals. How long is he going to let this go on for?

"A Great White Shark," says a girl sitting next to me.

We're including sea creatures now? Sharks aren't even mammals!

Mr. Melacki leans back against his desk. "I'll give everyone another hint. It's furry."

I doubt Mr. Melacki's latest clue will help. I can't think of an animal that doesn't have fur, except maybe a lizard.

As students continue to guess the name of the ship, I start to drift off, wondering what it would be like to sail my own ship across the Atlantic. I'm envious of the modern-day sailors who have sailed around the world by themselves. I heard it takes like four months. Talk about serious alone time! If I sailed around the world by myself, my talk-capacity would be so stocked up when I returned that I might come across as a regular person, at least for a week or so.

It's Mr. Melacki's latest clue that awakens me from my daydream. "I'll give you another hint. It likes to chew through wood and its name rhymes with cleaver."

Reagan leaps out of her seat. "The Termite!"

***

Over the past several days, I've noticed Reagan and Sophia spending more time with the popular kids in my class, although I think they're just loud.

Today, once again, Reagan and Sophia are summoned to the popular table during lunch. This will give Perry, Nate, and me a nice break, but it's made me realize something. Being popular isn't always about having the best personality. I've come to the conclusion that the louder someone is, the more popular they are. Since I'm quiet, I'm not considered that popular. Reagan and Sophia have been at my school for less than a week and they're already more popular than me. It doesn't seem fair. I've been here for two years and in the Virginia school system for seven. But it's true; more people know them and more teachers remember their names. And it's all because they're louder. That's it. That's the only reason. And the worst part is how loud kids are perceived compared to quiet kids. Loud kids are considered popular and energetic, but quiet kids are just quiet. This also explains why most popular kids don't get good grades. It's because they're busy talking and not studying.

I watch Reagan as she blabs away, and although I'm relieved that I'm not close enough to hear her, I know all of that blabbering will be directed at me as soon as I get home. Just the thought of it makes me tired. It's gotten so bad that I look forward to school. There's something seriously wrong with that!

"Perry, I need your help," I say.

"With what?"

"I can't handle Reagan anymore. She's destroying me one word at a time." I shake my head. "I'm going to end up like Nate."

Nate, who's slouched over his tray with his eyes half open, frowns.

I hold up a hand. "No offense, Nate."

He gives me a lethargic, understanding nod.

"And she thinks she's great at everything," I say to Perry, who taps his finger against his chin, thinking about it.

A minute later, his eyes brighten. "You need to convince her to go back to Texas."

"Really? How would I do that?"

"By finding her kryptonite."

I lift an eyebrow. "Her what?"

"Her kryptonite. Don't you read Superman? Kryptonite is Superman's one weakness. He becomes powerless if it comes near him."

"So I need to find Reagan's weakness?"

Perry leans forward. "Exactly. Everyone has one, including Superman, who by the way is an alien. Not many people realize that."

"So what do I do when I find her weakness?"

"Use it against her to get what you want. That's what Lex Luthor does."

***

Once a month, my Dad takes me to the local bookstore and lets me pick out a book. Hopefully it will be my first of three this month. As part of the bookstore's reading challenge, I'll get a free book if I can finish three by the end of May. Nate signed up with me.

Today, my dad let me bring Perry and Nate, which is good because Reagan invited herself, and it's easier on me when she has multiple people to talk to.

She stands with her arms folded as Perry, Nate and I browse the Science Fiction aisle. "This section's boring," she says. "All of the books are about stupid aliens and stupid monsters. Where are the real books?"

I turn away from the bookshelf and face her. "What do you consider a real book?"

"You know, books about awesome people, like big Joe Mufferaw."

I glance at Perry and Nate, then back at Reagan. "Who's big Joe Muffler ..."

"It's not *muffler*," she says. "It's *Mufferaw*."

"Who is he?" I ask.

"He was only the best lumberjack ever." She glances around the store. "Where's the lumberjack section in this store?"

"I don't think they have a section just for lumberjack books," Perry says.

An annoyed look fills Reagan's face. "Seriously? Bookstores in Virginia are terrible. Every bookstore in Texas has a lumberjack section."

"Try sports and recreation," I say, pointing across the store.

After she stomps off, we look at each other, giggle, and then continue scanning the shelf for books. I slide one off and read the back cover.

"Hey there, Colin," I hear someone say.

I know the voice. It's Sophia's. I just can't escape these loud girls.

"Hi, Sophia."

Her bright blue eyes settle on the book in my hands. "So you're picking out a book?"

"That's usually what I do when I come to the bookstore," I say.

"*Radioactive Jelly Beans*," she says, reading the cover. "Sounds sweet." She smiles wide. "Get it?"

Then she sees Perry and Nate. "Hi, guys."

"Hello," they both say.

"So have you read it?" she asks Perry.

"What?"

"*The Ninth Galaxy.* It just came out."

"Yes. Awesome."

It appears that Perry has learned from his last encounter with Sophia. He's conserving his talk-capacity by answering in as few words as possible. Nate uses this tactic a lot.

"I should be done with the book on Saturday," Sophia says.

"How do you know it'll be Saturday?" I ask.

"Because I read exactly one hour every day." She leans against the bookshelf and explains. "*The Ninth Galaxy* has two-hundred and twenty-five pages, and each page takes me approximately two minutes to complete ... I'm kind of a slow reader. So that works out to thirty pages a day. I stopped at page sixty yesterday, leaving me one-hundred and sixty-five pages to complete the book, which adds up to five and a half days. And since today is Tuesday, and I have yet to read today, I should be finished sometime on Saturday."

Perry and I stare at her, our mouths open.

"Her calculations are accurate," Nate says.

"Thanks," I say, and then turn to Sophia. "Did you just figure all that out in your head?"

"No, I have a schedule at home. Well, it's more of a calendar than a schedule. I like to know when I'm going to complete each book, so I can have another one ready to go."

Although I'm annoyed by Sophia's run-on explanation, I can't help but smile. Her quirkiness is refreshing for a loud person. Don't get me wrong, she's a talker for sure, but it's different than with Reagan. I don't get as tired listening to her.

Then I see Reagan striding toward us, and my jaw drops. She's cradling at least a dozen books in her arms.

"Reagan, we're only allowed to get one book each," I say.

"*One* book?" She pulls the books against her body. "No, I need all of these."

I take a step closer, examining the titles. "What did you get?"

"Well, aside from my lumberjack book, I have books on arm wresting, football, fishing, hunting, trucks, monster trucks, big monster trucks, extra big monster trucks, body building, rugby, and a book on the Boston Tea Party, because I think Mr. Melacki was wrong. I'm pretty sure one of the ships was called the termite. Plus, I'm a registered member of the tea party. If anyone would know about the Boston Tea Party, it would be a member of the tea party."

My Dad calls from the end of the aisle. "Are you guys ready?"

"Dad, Reagan picked out too many books," I say.

My Dad's eyes grow large when he sees the stack of books in Reagan's arms.

"Just one book please," my dad says to her.

She takes half of her books and sets them on a random shelf. "How about six? I really need these."

"How about one," my father says.

Reagan takes three more books off the top. "Three? One's on the Boston Tea Party, so it's educational."

"One?" my father says.

"Fine, I'll take this one," she says.

My father squints at the cover. "That's a limited edition copy, personally signed by the author. And it's ninety dollars."

47

"But it's about my favorite lumberjack," Reagan says.

"The cost is approximately five hundred percent more than your average book," says Nate.

"Who asked you?" says Reagan.

"Nobody," he says. "I volunteered the information."

I nudge Nate. "What do you think the chances are my dad buys it for her?"

"What does your dad do for a living?" Nate asks.

"He's an electrical engineer," I say.

"Six percent," Nate says.

Reagan looks to my father, still hopeful.

"Sorry, Reagan, but you'll have to pick another book. It's too expensive."

"Fine," says Reagan, shaking her head. "But it's not going to be an educational book."

***

Later that afternoon, Violet and I decide to play tennis. It's a good excuse to leave the house and escape from Reagan.

I bounce the tennis ball three times and then peer over the net at Violet, who's in a crouched position, awaiting my serve. I toss the ball in the air, then bring my racquet high over my head, powering through it. Violet reaches to her right and makes contact, hitting a forehand high over the net. I raise my hand as her shot sails a few inches past the baseline. Violet does this too. Raising our hands allows us to indicate that the ball was long without having to scream 'out' fifty times a match.

We also don't announce the score after each point because that can add up to a lot of words. We keep score in our head. It was Violet's idea and it's a good one. I mean as long as you're paying attention, announcing the score after each point just isn't necessary.

"That was in," I hear a voice call from outside the fence.

I look over my shoulder and see Reagan, one hand gripping the chain link fence and the other holding my mother's tennis racquet.

"It caught the line," she says, pointing through the fence.

"It was like three inches out," I say.

Reagan shakes her head. "I think you need glasses."

I roll my eyes, and then turn and face her. "What are you doing?"

She waves her racquet. "Hello, I'm holding a tennis racquet. What do you think I'm doing?"

"But I'm playing Violet," I say.

"Not anymore," she says, looking past me.

I glance across the net, but don't see Violet. Then I spot her sprinting down the sidewalk toward our house.

"She's weird," Reagan says.

"Violet is *not* weird," I say.

Reagan comes through the gate and onto the court. "She sure seems weird to me."

I squeeze the handle of my racquet. "Well she's not."

She jogs past me, taking her position on the other side of the net.

I tap the strings of my racquet against my head. "I guess this means we're playing ..."

Reagan bounces from foot to foot, twirling the racquet in her hand.

I hold up a ball. "Do you want to warm up first?"

"Warming up is for wimps. Just serve."

There's probably no need to mention then that Violet and I warmed up for thirty-five minutes.

I pull a ball from my pocket and bounce it three times. I crack a hard serve, but Reagan gets the ball back. We exchange a few volleys and then her fourth shot drifts long. I raise my hand.

Reagan stands, her racquet resting on her shoulder. "What does that mean?"

"What does what mean?" I ask.

She holds her hand in the air, imitating me. "When you raise your hand. What is that?"

"It means the ball's out."

"Why don't you just say *out*?"

I lift my shoulders. "I don't know, it just seems easier."

"Well it's not," she says. "Just say it. And by the way, I don't think it was out. You definitely need glasses."

My eyes narrow. "It was out, Reagan."

"Well at least you said it this time," she says.

I walk back to the service line, wipe sweat from my forehead, and then bounce the ball three times.

"Why do you always bounce the ball three times?" she calls from across the court.

I hold the ball, looking at it in my hand. "That's just what I do. It's my serving routine."

"Your serving routine is annoying."

I exhale, and bounce the ball three times. Again.

"Annoying ..." I hear her say.

I serve, but she hits the return right past me, just inside the line. I scoop up two loose balls, stuff one in my pocket, and prepare to serve with the other.

"Wait, what's the score?" Reagan says.

"Fifteen fifteen," I say.

Her forehead wrinkles in confusion.

It takes me ten minutes to explain the scoring. When I'm done, my head is pounding as if I've been hit in the face by a thousand tennis balls. I've only played two points and I'm worn out.

I lose the set 6-0.

"Game, net, *and* match," Reagan says, after my final shot hits the net.

"It's *set*," I say. "Not net."

Reagan doesn't hear me and whacks a tennis ball into the air, celebrating her victory. "Bam!"

Although she's only won a set and not an entire match, I don't argue that it's over. It would be too exhausting to finish.

Then she gallops around the court pumping her fist in the air. After three gallops around, she struts toward me at the net, her head rocking back and forth. "I am the champion of tennis."

"Whatever," I say.

"You're just going to have to get used to it, Colin."

"Get used to what?"

"Losing. Because every time you play against me, no matter what the game, no matter what the sport, you're going to lose."

"You just got lucky," I say.

"Lucky? Please. I've never played tennis before in my life and I crushed you."

"I can beat you at stuff too, even stuff you're good at."

She starts to laugh. "Like what!"

"I don't know ... what are you good at?"

"I'm good at everything."

I look down at the ground. "The only thing you're good at is talking."

"First of all, talking isn't a game. Second of all, even if it was, I would absolutely destroy you."

"Yeah, right ..."

"Then do it," she says.

"Do what?" I ask.

"Out talk me."

"How? We can't make talking a game."

"We don't have to. It already is a game. It's called the debate team."

I step toward her, gripping the top of the net. "You want me to join your debate team and ... *debate* you?"

"Not my team," she says. "We're already full. But the other team needs someone."

I think about what Reagan said. This might be the opportunity that Perry mentioned. Over-confidence is Reagan's kryptonite. She thinks she can beat me at anything, so much that she might be willing to bet on it, and bet big.

"Okay," I say.

She licks her lips, thinking about it. "So what does the winner get?"

"What do you want?"

"I want your room. I'm tired of sleeping on the couch. I want a room with a bed."

I swallow. This is big. My room is my sanctuary, and if I lose that, I lose my recharging station, the one place I'm guaranteed to be alone.

I can't do it.

"No ... it ... it has to be something else. I ..."

"It's your room or nothing."

Sweat drips down my face as I think about losing my room. But Reagan's not going to settle for anything less. It's a huge risk, but it's my only chance.

"Fine," I say. I wipe my face dry. "If you win, you can stay in my room for as long as you're here."

She cocks her head to the side. "Okay, so what do you want if you win? Although I can't believe I'm asking because it's never going to happen."

I tilt my head up, looking her right in the eye. "I want you to go back to Texas."

"*What*?"

"If I beat you in the debate, I want you to tell your parents that you miss them so much, you want to go back to Texas and wait for them to sell their house."

She snorts. "That's ridiculous. But whatever, it doesn't matter. You're never going to beat me in a debate."

"So when's the debate?"

"In four weeks." She leans over the net, her beefy nose rubbing against mine. "I'm going to talk so much during our debate, your ears are going to fall off. You're going down, Colin Quigley."

CHAPTER 4

FIRE DRILL

I pace across Perry's bedroom, breathing heavily. "I can't believe what I've done."

"You can do this," Perry says.

My heart is thumping. "How? She'll destroy me. She talks way too much."

There's a knock at the door and Nate enters.

"Where have you been?" I ask, rubbing my sweaty palms.

"I had trouble understanding your message," says Nate. "You were screaming."

"Of course I was screaming! I'm going to lose my room!"

Nate stares at me. "You bet *your room*?"

"Yes," I say, shutting my eyes.

"Why?" Nate says. "I would give anything to have my own room."

"This isn't helping, Nate." I look to Perry. "What am I going to do?"

He closes the door, and then leans against it, thinking. "Can you get out of the bet?" he asks. "Just say they wouldn't take you on the debate team."

I shake my head. "I already tried that this morning. Reagan said if I don't make the team, then I automatically lose the bet."

"There's an eighty-six percent chance you'll make the team," says Nate.

"No way," says Perry, shaking his head. "That seems high."

"That does seem high, Nate. Why are you so confident I'll make the team?" I ask.

"My brother Dexter's the team captain," says Nate. "He said he'd take anyone."

"Why anyone?" asks Perry.

"Because no one has volunteered," says Nate.

Perry grins. "I'm not surprised Dexter's on the team," he says. "Kids who join are usually talkers. And I've heard about these debates. Pretty much whoever talks the most, wins."

I throw my arms in the air. "Wonderful. I'm going to get slaughtered."

"That's true," says Nate. "You probably will."

"Is there anything good you can tell me, Nate?"

"Yes."

"And that would be …"

"Only one percent of the student body attends the debates," he says. "They're not very popular."

I sink onto Perry's bed, staring at the floor.

"So what do you think my odds of winning are?" I ask him.

He doesn't answer.

"*Nate.* Just tell me. What are the odds of me beating Reagan in a debate?"

"Point zero zero … zero … zero zero… zero … zero zero zero one."

"So is that like one percent?" I ask.

"No."

I squeeze my hands together. "What it is?"

"It's a billionth of a percent," says Nate.

"And that's worse?"

"Yes."

I hunch over. "I think those are the worst odds you've ever given me."

"Yes."

"I think those are the worst odds you've ever given anything."

"Yes."

***

As students shuffle down the stairs at the end of the day, I squeeze past them, heading up. When I reach the second floor, I walk down the hall to room 204, where a sign on the door reads: DEBATE PRACTICE.

I knock and step inside.

"Hey, Colin," says Dexter, a big smile on his face.

Dexter's at the chalkboard, standing next to an eighth grader named Todd.

"Are you looking for Nate?" Dexter asks.

"No … I'm here to see you."

He brushes chalk from his hands. "Sure, what can I do for you?"

"I … uh … wanted to see if there was still an opening on your debate team."

Todd laughs.

"What's so funny?" I ask.

"You're quiet," he says.

Two-hundred and eighty-five.

"So?"

He looks to Dexter and then to me. "Quiet kids don't usually join the debate team. You know, because they're at a disadvantage."

"What disadvantage?"

"They don't talk much," Todd says. "And you need to talk a lot to win a debate."

Dexter raises his hand. "Hold on. Let's clarify what he's asking, like any good debater should do." He moves toward me. "Colin simply asked if there was an opening, not that he wanted to join. Maybe he was asking for a friend."

"No … it's me," I say. "I want to join."

Dexter stops in front of me. "Okay, so is this a good time for an interview?"

I shuffle my feet. "I have to interview for it?"

"Is that a problem?" asks Todd.

"No …"

"We just want to make sure you're a good fit for the team, and that the team's a good fit for you," says Dexter.

"I guess that's fine," I say, but wishing I had time to prepare.

Dexter and Todd take two seats in the first row and have me stand in front of them. My knees wobble as Dexter begins to talk.

"Now I know this can be a little intimidating, but we like to do it this way, so we can see your potential as a debater." He pauses. "Are you ready?"

I give a tense nod.

"You don't want to nod or shake your head in a debate," says Todd. "You should answer verbally so the judges are clear on your response. Does that make sense?"

I nod.

Todd taps his fingers against the desk as if he's waiting for something.

"Oh," I say. "Yes."

"Was that a yes for starting the interview or for acknowledging that you shouldn't nod?" asks Todd.

My hands start to shake and I grip them behind my back. "I'm not sure."

"Let's go ahead and start," says Dexter, then clears his throat. "Tell us why you want to be on the debate team."

"I have to," I say. "Otherwise I'll lose my room, and if that happens I might die."

Dexter and Todd glance at each other.

"Very well," says Dexter. "Why do you think you'd be a good debater?"

"Um ... I think ... I could maybe win ... a debate."

Dexter interlocks his fingers, resting his hands against the desk. "And what makes you think you could win a debate? What sort of skills do you have that would allow you to debate successfully?"

"What skills do I have?" I ask.

"That's correct," says Dexter. "And nice job clarifying the question by the way."

I smile, relax my shoulders, and let my hands fall to my side. "Thanks."

They both stare at me for a long moment.

"Do you want me to repeat the question?" asks Dexter.

My hands begin trembling again. "Oh … sure."

Todd raises his voice. "What skills do you have?"

"Uh … I'm good at Wii. And I have a good left-footed shot in soccer."

"That's great, Colin," says Dexter. "But what skills do you have that would make you a good debater?"

I squeeze my hands together. "Can you repeat the question?"

Dexter holds up a hand. "Let's move to another one. What benefits could you gain from being on the debate team?"

"Oh, I know," I say.

Dexter and Todd lean forward in their seats.

"I could win my room back, and then I wouldn't die."

"Well, we're looking for things like … learning the art of persuasion, developing better research skills, improving your public speaking …" says Dexter.

I swallow. "Okay," I say, my body stiff. "I would learn the art of persuasion, develop better research skills, and improve my public speaking."

Dexter looks at Todd. "What do you think? I really like him."

***

When I walk through my front door an hour later, Reagan is waiting. "So did you interview for the debate position?" she asks.

"Yeah," I say, closing the door.

She rubs her hands together as if she's about to open a gift. "And they told you to scram, right? I have your room now?"

"No," I say, holding my chin high. "I made the team."

Her mouth falls open. "You're kidding."

"Nope. Nailed the interview."

After taking my seat on the bus on Monday morning, I notice that Reagan hasn't followed me down the aisle.

She's talking with another boy several rows up. It's about time she ruined someone else's morning.

As the bus pulls away, she sits down next to him. I actually feel sorry for the boy. He has no idea how much talking she's capable of. Maybe this will become a routine for the two of them. Wouldn't that be great? I'll be doing plenty of talking to prepare for the debate, so I could use a break in the mornings.

The bus stops again and Sophia gets on, taking the seat in front of me.

"Hi, Colin," she says.

I give her a wave. It's a nice alternative to saying 'hi.'

She taps her seat, eager to say something. "Reagan told me about your debate."

"What did she say?" I ask.

"Well … let's just say Reagan's pretty confident she's going to win."

I stare at her. "Is that what you think?"

Sophia cranes her neck toward me. "No."

"You're just being nice," I say, my eyes falling to the ground.

"Well if I didn't think you had a chance, then why would I come watch?" Sophia says.

I feel my stomach clench. "You're going to watch the debate?"

She nods. "A few of my friends are going, too."

"Why? No one goes to those things."

Sophia shrugs. "I don't know, I think they find this one interesting. You against Reagan, the introvert against the extrovert."

I don't consider *introvert* as offensive as *quiet*, so I decide not to increase my total. I'm still at two-hundred and eighty-five.

Then a loud voice pierces my ear.

"Scoot over."

I look up and see a gigantic mouth staring me in the face. I don't have to look past the mouth to see who it is; only Reagan has a mouth that big. It took her less than two minutes to take him out. The poor boy never had a chance.

"What's up Sophia?" says Reagan, and then surprises her with a fist bump.

Sophia shakes her hand. "Ow."

"That's not good," Reagan says, grabbing Sophia's hand as she sits down.

"I'll be okay," Sophia says.

"No, I'm talking about your lifeline," says Reagan.

"My what?"

"Your lifeline." Reagan turns Sophia's hand so it's facing her. "This right here is your lifeline." She traces a line on Sophia's palm that goes from the top of her wrist to just below her index finger.

"So? What's the big deal?" asks Sophia.

"The big deal is that yours doesn't go very far. It should go all the way to your index finger." Reagan points to a spot on Sophia's hand. "Yours only goes to here."

"And what does that mean?" asks Sophia.

"It means that you won't live very long," says Reagan.

Sophia examines her hand. "What? How long is the line?"

"An inch ... *maybe*," says Reagan. "If I had to guess, you'll die when you're about twelve."

Sophia looks up from her hand. "But I'm twelve now."

"It should be any day then. Probably Thursday."

"I'm going to die on Thursday?" Sophia asks with laugh.

Reagan shrugs. "Give or take a day. I'd say Thursday or Friday."

"Let me see Colin's hand," Sophia says, taking my hand. Her eyes widen. "Wow, look at that." She moves her finger along my lifeline. "That's long. Looks like you'll live to be about a hundred and fifty."

I'm surprised it's so long. I thought the debate would have shortened my lifespan. As Sophia's finger slides along my palm, my heart starts thumping and I feel knots in my stomach. I think I'm getting sick.

Although it's a relief when we reach school, the day doesn't start well. In math, I hear the sound that frightens all quiet kids. The fire alarm. Oh, the dreaded fire alarm.

Most kids like fire alarms because they get to go outside for awhile. I can't stand them. Every time I hear the fire alarm, I cringe. And it's not because I think there's a fire, although that would be bad. It's because I'll need to talk and it takes so much energy to start a random conversation.

I could stand off by myself, but then I'd feel like an outcast. I would rather stay in class than participate in a fire drill. In class, I'm not allowed to talk, which works great for me, but there's no such rule during a fire drill, so I feel obligated.

After my class exits the school, I glance around, wondering which student I'll have to exchange useless small-talk with. Then I notice Ronald Winkler standing by himself. I'm actually surprised we're not friends yet.

He already has the most important quality I'm looking for in a friend, and aside from the lack of variety in Ronald's clothing, he seems pretty normal.

I'm certain Ronald won't initiate a conversation, so I walk over, and as I do, I see Larry and Stanley Botchaway approaching him. They're on Reagan's debate team and live next door to me.

Larry points at the same brown, button-down shirt Ronald has worn for the past few weeks. "You know, Einstein used to where the same shirt every day, too."

"Yes, but Einstein had several shirts," says Stanley, sliding his hands into his pants. "They were just all the same."

Ronald takes a few awkward steps back.

"So that's the question," says Larry. "Do you wear the same shirt every day or are all your shirts the same? I suspect there's just one."

"Hey, guys," I say, interrupting.

Larry's eyes shift to me. "Well, if it isn't our neighbor, Master Quigley."

"It's ... Colin," I say.

Larry chuckles and puts a hand over his chest. "My mistake."

"No problem," I say. "It happens all the time."

"We hear you've joined the other debate team," says Stanley.

"Yup."

"*Yup?*" Larry says with a smirk. "I imagine you'll be quite the foe."

I scrunch my nose up, confused. "Is foe like an opponent?"

Larry nods. "It is, but don't feel bad you didn't know. It's a tough word."

"It's not that tough," I say. "It's not like pneumonia."

"Still, we'll ask Reagan not to use either during the debate," Stanley says. "We wouldn't want to confuse you."

"I'll be fine," I say, folding my arms.

"Of course you will," Larry says, grinning as he and Stanley begin to stroll away. "And can you ask your family to keep it down next door. You're quite noisy."

"Don't listen to those guys," I say to Ronald. "They're jerks." I take a step closer. "I'm Colin. We're in a couple classes together."

He looks at me and his hands start to shake. "Err … "

It's just what I thought. He's quiet *and* shy, and there's a difference. Just because someone is quiet, doesn't mean they're shy. I don't consider myself shy. It's just that the *act* of talking wears me out.

So I decide to take an approach that would work with me. A simple question to get things started.

"Do you like to read?" I ask.

"I—I—I like books." He kicks at the pavement. "I've b—been reading ... *Radioactive Jelly Beans*."

"Me too!" I say, smiling. "Isn't it awesome."

"Yeah, like—like when they grew really tall after eating the b—b—blue jelly beans."

"Or when their hair fell out after eating the malachite ones?" I say.

"It's p—p—pronounced mala-*kite*."

"It is?"

"Yeah. B—But it's okay. It's a r—r—rare color."

Ronald smiles, and is starting to look more comfortable. He moves toward me, but then stops, his eyes bulging wide.

"Hey," a girl's voice says.

It's Sophia. I attempt to introduce Ronald, but he's gone. I think he's terrified of girls.

I would prefer not to talk to Sophia because I know the conversation would be much more draining than the one with Ronald, and I also hate blowing my talk-capacity on one person. Not to mention, I already talked to Sophia on the bus. What more could she possibly have to say?

"So this is a drill, right?" Sophia asks. "There's no fire?"

This is another pet peeve of mine: two consecutive questions, one of which has a 'yes' answer and the other a 'no.' This requires an enormous amount of energy to handle because you can't answer with one word. You have to answer, but then also explain which question it's for.

So just to confuse her, I answer with one word.

"No."

"Great," she says.

I scratch my head and stare at her. "Wait, how do you know which question I was answering? "I might have just said, '*No*, this isn't a drill.'"

"You were answering the second question," she says.

"But how do you know that?"

"Because if someone asks two questions in a row, and you only give one answer, it should always be for the second question."

"Really? I didn't know that."

"Yeah, and sorry about that by the way. I try to avoid asking two questions in a row that could have opposite one-word answers. I know it's annoying."

Sophia looks past me and spots Ronald, who's standing by himself under a light pole.

"I hope I didn't scare him," she says.

"He's a little shy around girls," I say.

She moves closer, the corners of her lips curling up. "Are you shy around girls?"

"Only when they talk a lot."

"Okay ... well how about we just stand here and enjoy each other's company. No talking for the rest of the fire drill."

I roll my eyes.

"You don't think I can do it, do you?" she asks.

I hold back a laugh and shake my head.

She spreads her feet apart, straightening her body. "I'll bet you a bag of pretzels that I can go the rest of the fire drill without saying a single word."

I grin. "You'll never be able to last that long."

"So do we have a bet?" she asks.

Over the past few years, I've noticed something. It's just as hard for a loud person *not* to talk as it is for a quiet person to talk, so I'm pretty confident that I'll win the bag of pretzels.

I nod, agreeing to the bet. Sophia folds her arms and presses her lips together.

She'll last all of eight seconds.

Two minutes go by. It has to be killing her not to talk.

A few more minutes and still nothing. She's about to explode, I know it. The words are about to start flying, so I take a step back. I don't want to get hit when this happens. But Sophia just smiles back at me, looking calm and content.

After ten minutes of silence, I try to tempt her. "Wow, it sure feels good to talk. It gives me so much energy. This is great."

Not a peep. Sophia couldn't look more relaxed. If the lack of talking is affecting her, she sure is hiding it well.

When she reaches thirteen minutes, I try to cut my losses. "Okay, okay, let's call it even. You can talk and no has to lose any pretzels."

She shakes her head. No deal.

A few minutes later, Principle Reiland announces that the fire drill is over and we can return to our classes. Sophia goes a full sixteen and a half minutes without saying a peep. For a loud person, she sure has a lot of self-control.

***

My next class is history and Mr. Melacki has asked us to separate into groups.

"Nothing like a little group activity to help stimulate the old noggin," he says.

I'm not sure what a noggin is, but it sounds like a head. I actually thought it was a nose, but that wouldn't make sense. Even if it does stimulate my noggin, I don't like separating into groups. I'm afraid that no one will choose me, and although I could be the one that chooses, I'd be embarrassed if the person said no. Not to mention, I have to be careful not to get stuck with a talker.

Ronald is probably my safest choice, but as I'm about to ask him, I hear Reagan say, "Colin and the weird kid, you two are with me."

She drags her desk across the floor, positions it so it's facing mine, and then reaches over and grabs hold of Ronald's desk. With him still in it and his hands clutching the sides like he's on a roller coaster, Reagan swings Ronald over. His desk slams into mine.

We're supposed to work as a group to come up with three reasons why the colonies declared their independence from England. Mr. Melacki lets us use our textbooks, so Ronald and I pull ours from our backpacks and begin scanning the chapters.

Then I hear Reagan drumming her fingers against her desk.

"What are you doing?" I ask. "And where's your book? Mr. Melacki said we could use them."

She extends her arms into the air, stretching. "I didn't bring it."

"Again. Why not?"

"I don't really need it," she says. "Plus I saw a movie about the Civil War once."

"Our assignment is on the Revolutionary War."

Reagan crosses her feet under her desk and leans back. "It doesn't matter. I do better when I don't prepare. That's why I'm going to crush you in the debate."

I look over to Ronald, who's holding his book an inch from his face. I'm not sure if he's reading or just avoiding eye contact.

"You're going to d—debate Reagan?" he says from behind his book.

I cover my face and nod.

"I—I—I'd like to watch that," he says.

"Well don't be late," says Reagan. "I'm going to knock him out in the first thirty seconds."

"Let's talk about the assignment," I say. "We still need a plan."

"Why do we need a plan?" she says.

I turn my palms up. "So we know what we're going to say when Mr. Melacki calls on us."

"You're definitely not going to do well in the debate," she says. "And don't worry about the assignment. I'll go for us."

Ronald lowers his book slightly, his eyes meeting mine. I can tell from his expression that he's thinking the same thing as me. What is this girl going to say when it's our turn to go?

"Why don't you let Ronald and me write down a few things ... and then you can just read it," I say.

"Nah, I'm good," she says.

To be safe, I spend the next five minutes reading about the Declaration of Independence and what led up to it. As I read, I start drifting again, wondering how I could declare my own independence from Reagan. I'd start by writing a constitution, which would go something like, 'Me, the kid in Virginia, in order to form a more quiet union, establish silence, insure limited domestic talking, and promote quiet time, do establish this Constitution for ... uh ... me.'

"Okay, who would like to go first?" I hear Mr. Melacki say, startling me.

Reagan's hand goes up. "We'll go." Her eyes drift to the ceiling as she thinks about what to say. "What was the topic again?"

I drop my face into my hands.

"You're supposed to ..." Mr. Melacki says, and then pauses.

When I look up, I see him scratching his chin, a confused look on his face. Don't tell me he's forgotten too.

"Oh, right," he says. "You're supposed to come up with three reasons why the colonies declared their independence."

Ronald keeps the book against his face.

"Number one," says Reagan, holding up an index finger. "Taxation without compensation."

Representation.

She holds up both of her index fingers. "Number two. The green tea that the East Indiana trading company brought us, tasted terrible."

East India. And it did?

"And number three."

This time she holds up three fingers on *each* hand. Technically this is six, but I don't say anything since she's doing the talking for us.

"The colonists didn't like that their green tea was being delivered by a ship called the termite," she says. "I'm *positive* that was one of the ship's names."

Mr. Melacki presses his hands together, taking in her responses. I sit there, holding my breath, completely still.

"So who wants to go next?" Mr. Melacki says.

That's it? He's not going to comment on any of her reasons? What if the class thinks she's right?

Reagan looks over at me, a satisfying grin spreading across her face. "I told you I had it."

***

Later that week, I invite Perry over to play Swordplay Duel on my Wii. He arrives wearing an army helmet and a camouflage shirt.

"Wow, you're taking this seriously," I say.

"If you look the part, you will play the part," Perry says, and then takes a swig of his soda.

My parents said I could start drinking soda when I turned twelve, and although my twelfth birthday was a few months ago, I still haven't tried one. Perry tends to talk more after he's had a few sodas. He's bearable after one or two, but once he starts on his third, he goes on an ugly talking spree. My mom is the same way with coffee, and this concerns me about my relationship with Perry when we get older. I'll need to monitor his drinking as our game progresses.

He steps inside, keeping his voice low. "Is Reagan here?"

My lips curl up. "The house is Reagan-free."

"Where is she?" he says, closing the door.

"She's playing football with some high school kids."

"Those poor boys." Perry shakes his head. "I can't imagine what it's like to live with her."

"It's pretty much the worst thing in the world," I say.

"I don't know how you're going to beat her in a debate," says Perry.

My stomach wrenches with the thought of losing my room.

Perry takes another drink. "I'll be honest though, I can't wait to see it."

"You're going?" I ask.

"Yeah, I'm going with Nate," Perry says.

"Why would Nate want to see a debate?"

Perry lifts his shoulders. "I think he considers it an experiment. He wants to know what happens when a quiet kid talks too much."

I wonder if I could really die from this?

"You know, if things start going bad during the debate," Perry says, "you may want to pour water on her."

"Why?"

"Because she might be an alien, and if she is, water might destroy her. I saw this movie once where you could destroy the aliens by pouring water on them."

Perry hasn't even finished his soda, but he's already starting to talk more. I sigh, tired from our conversation, then lead him to the basement. After we turn on the Wii console, Perry pulls a green mask from his pocket and hands it to me.

"What's this?" I ask, holding it up.

"It's an alien mask."

The mask has wide eyes, a tiny mouth, and a massive, padded forehead covered in purple veins.

"You want me to wear this?" I ask.

He nods. "Yeah, is that cool?"

I stretch the mask, looking inside the eyeholes. "I don't know, it seems kind of strange."

Perry puts his hand on my shoulder. "It will help me prepare, Colin."

"Prepare for what?"

"For when I fight the aliens."

"Okay, okay," I say.

Then we hear a loud snoring behind us. Perry looks over his shoulder and sees someone sleeping on the couch.

"ZZZ-zzzzz …"

"Who's that?" Perry asks.

"It's Nate," I say, pulling the mask over my head.

"Yeah, that happens to him at my house, too."

"ZZZ-zzzzz-ZZzzz-PPPppp …"

Perry adjusts the strap on his plastic army helmet, then grips his Wii remote. The game starts and Perry's Mii comes after mine. I block the first few shots, and then my Mii swings from left to right, sending his stumbling back. My next swing, a huge uppercut, knocks him from the platform and he plummets into the water below. Or it might be lava, I'm not sure.

"ZZZ-zzzzz-ZZzzz-GGgggg-rgppp …"

His Mii charges again and we exchange blows to the body as the crowd cheers. I back him to the edge of the platform, slashing him across the chest. He tumbles to his death.

Perry rips off his helmet and chucks it on the floor. "*Looking the part* doesn't work." He drops his shoulders. "I'm not going to be ready when they invade."

Then we hear a loud cackling behind us. The house is no longer Reagan-free. She's standing in the doorway, holding a football helmet in one hand and clutching her stomach with the other as she continues to laugh.

"What's so funny?" I ask.

"You're playing Wii and wearing an alien mask," she says. "You need to get out more."

I pull off the mask and pat my hair down. "What's wrong with playing Wii?"

Reagan drops the helmet, then moves toward us, her big feet thumping against the floor as she walks. "Because it's fake."

"Wii games are very realistic," Perry says.

"No they're not," Reagan says. "And I can prove it."

"How?" I ask.

Her hands move to her hips. "How many times have you played that game?"

"I don't know," I say. "Like a hundred."

"Okay, so you've played a hundred times—although it's probably more like five-hundred—and I've played zero. But if we had a real swordfight, I would destroy you."

I fold my arms over my chest. "No, you wouldn't."

"Then let's duel."

"What ..."

Her eyes narrow. "Let's duel."

"Reagan, my mom's not going to let us fight with real swords."

Perry points to the toy shelf in the corner of my basement. "You could use your Star Wars lightsabers."

"That'll work," says Reagan.

As she walks back to get them, I glare at Perry.

"Sorry," he says. "Do you want to use my helmet?"

I frown. "You mean because it helped you so much?"

"Here," Reagan says, handing me a lightsaber. Then she raises hers above her head, preparing to strike me.

I hold my palm up, leaning back. "Wait, wait, wait. I need to ... get ready or something."

She lowers her lightsaber. "Get ready for what?"

"For the fight," I say, backing away from her. "I need to be mentally ready."

"You're weird," she says. "I feel sorry for your debate coach."

I bite down on my lip. "I'm not weird."

"ZZZ-Zzzz-ZZzzz …"

Reagan turns toward the couch, pointing at Nate with her lightsaber. "There's a homeless guy sleeping on your coach."

"It's not a homeless guy," I say. "It's Nate."

"ZZZ-Zzzz-ZZzzz-kkkhngPpphhhh-Zzzzz . . ."

"Do you have any normal friends?" she asks.

"I have an idea," Perry says. "Why don't you guys stand with your backs against each other, then walk ten steps."

"That's stupid, but fine," says Reagan. "Will that make you *mentally* ready?"

I nod. "Yeah, that should do it."

Reagan and I turn, pressing our backs to one another. She's a full head taller than me and I can feel the sweat from her back against my neck.

I suck in a long breath, exhale, and then begin to walk away from her, kicking my feet high as I move. After ten steps, we turn and face each other. Reagan has a hardened look on her face, her eyes steady. We flip on our lightsabers, brightening the basement. My hands shake as I raise my lightsaber into the air. Reagan holds hers in front of her, angling it across her face. She looks like a Japanese swordsman, but bigger.

Then she charges toward me with her mouth open, screaming. I block the first few shots, but I can't keep up. Reagan is grunting and swinging like we're in an actual sword fight.

Oh wait, we are in an actual sword fight.

Then her sword slashes across my stomach.

"Fatal shot!" says Perry, pointing at my belly. "You're out!"

Reagan smirks and lowers her lightsaber. "*See.*"

I look down. "That's one time."

"You only get once chance in a real sword fight, Colin." She pokes me with her lightsaber. "But I'd be happy to thrash you again if you want."

I look to Perry. It's time to put our fire drill skills to good use.

Evacuate! Evacuate!

CHAPTER 5
PRACTICE

After school on Wednesday, I meet Dexter and Todd in the same classroom where I had the interview. This will be my first practice session with my team.

I slide into a desk as Dexter walks to the chalkboard.

"Our school uses a debate style called SPAR," he says, writing each letter on the board. "It stands for spontaneous argumentation."

I doubt I'll like a debate style that has the word spontaneous in it.

"The SPAR debate pairs two debaters against each other," says Todd. "So although we'll be judged as a team, we won't be debating as one. You're going to be on your own out there."

I guess that's good. I do like to be alone.

"The moderator will provide the topic twenty minutes before the debate starts and you'll have that time to prepare," says Dexter.

"So what happens after twenty minutes?" I ask.

Todd scratches his head. "You debate."

"You mean I won't be able to go home and get ready or anything?" I ask.

"That's why they call it spontaneous argumentation," Todd says.

I knew I wasn't going to like it.

Dexter leaves the chalkboard and walks toward me. "You'll be debating three topics against your opponent."

"Like … one for each of us?"

"No," says Todd. "Three *each*."

I'm definitely not going to like this.

"Now it varies for each debate," says Dexter, "but usually each topic will last about ten to fifteen minutes, so your entire debate session, not including preparation time, will last anywhere from thirty to forty-five minutes."

I swallow. "So I might have to talk for forty-five minutes straight?"

"Is that a problem?" asks Todd.

Yes, that's a huge problem. I've never even had to talk for ten minutes straight.

"I guess not …" I say.

Dexter sits on the teacher's desk. "Our school has two debate teams. Your cousin's team name is Kiss My Rebuttal."

"That's good," I say, giggling. "What's our name?"

"The Debate Team," says Dexter.

I turn my ear toward him. "What?"

"The Debate Team."

"Our debate team name is … 'The Debate Team?'" I ask.

"Correct. I wanted something simple that wouldn't offend anyone," says Dexter. "Now, each team has three members. Todd will be debating Stanley, I'll be debating Larry, and you're going against Reagan. I hear she's quite good, so I want you to begin debating right away."

My heart begins to thump.

"We'll start you with a debate against Todd," says Dexter. "It may be a little awkward since it's your first time, but it'll be good practice."

"Okay," I say, peeking over at Todd.

"And I'm going to serve as the moderator," says Dexter.

"What's the topic going to be?" I ask.

Dexter moves to the chalkboard and begins writing. "Students should work during high school." He faces us. "Todd will argue for and Colin will argue against."

"So Colin," Todd says to me, "that means I'll give reasons why I think students *should* work in high school and you'll give reasons why they shouldn't."

Dexter checks his watch. "But first, each of you will have twenty minutes to prepare. There are newspapers, magazines, and journals on the desks next to you. They all have articles related to this topic." He pushes a button on his watch. "Ready, set, …"

I hold up a finger. "Wait, can I have extra time to prepare?"

"You will," says Dexter. "You'll have twenty minutes. That's the timer I'm about to start."

"I know, but I need like … extra extra time."

Dexter looks at me, confused. "You'll have time. You'll have twenty minutes."

"No, I need time to get ready for the preparation," I say.

"You need preparation time for your preparation time?" asks Todd.

I nod. "Sort of."

"How much time do you need?" asks Dexter.

"I don't know, like five minutes."

"But not to look through the articles?" asks Dexter.

"No."

Dexter looks at Todd, and then presses a few buttons on his watch. "Okay, since this is your first time, we'll give you five minutes of preparation time … before you begin your twenty minutes of preparation time."

I smile. "Thanks."

"Okay, your five minutes of pre-preparation time, starts now," says Dexter.

After his watch beeps, Dexter and Todd stare at me. I take a few longs breaths and just sit there as Todd taps his foot against the floor.

A minute later, I say, "Okay, I think that's enough."

"So you're ready to start the actual preparation time?" asks Dexter.

I nod. "Oh, sorry, *yes*."

Dexter sets his watch again and says, "Start now."

Within the first minute, I see Todd flipping through magazines and scribbling on index cards, turning one over after another.

I sit up and stretch my neck forward, squinting at his cards. He looks up at me, his eyes narrowing.

"What are you doing?" he asks. "Are you looking at my notes?"

I snap my head back. "No …"

"Yes you were," he says. "You were cheating."

"I was just … checking out your knuckles," I say.

Todd holds his hands out in front of him. "Why would you check out my knuckles?"

I shrug. "Well … you got some real nice knuckles."

Then I flip through one of the journals and immediately begin writing as if I know exactly what to write down, but what I'm actually writing is 'I have no idea what to write down.'

Once the twenty minutes is up, Dexter motions to Todd. "Todd, you're going to start. Again, the topic is 'students should work during high school.' Todd will argue for and Colin will argue against."

Todd sits up in his desk, organizing his index cards.

"Begin," says Dexter.

"The skills acquired from students working are invaluable," Todd says. "Working while you're a student teaches you time management, responsibility, self reliance, and provides a strong work ethic, not to mention actual working experience."

Dexter's eyes shift to me.

"Uh … not working is better … because you'd get really tired," I say. "Especially if you worked at a fast food place and had to take everyone's order, and then repeat the orders back to them. All that talking would make you really tired and probably hurt your grades."

"Again, it gets back to time management," Todd says. "Having a job forces you to go to bed earlier. That way you won't get *tired*," he says, shooting me a look, "taking fast food orders at your job."

"Even if I went to bed earlier, I'd still be tired if I had to repeat everyone's order," I say.

Todd begins to say something, but Dexter holds up his hand, stopping him. "Colin, try to counter using something from your notes."

"Oh right," I say, having completely forgotten about my research.

Remembering a counter argument I had written down, I lean over my paper, scanning for it. "Oh here it is." I clear my throat and read. "Colleges look at grades, not job experience. So a job would not increase your chances of being accepted at a college and would also reduce the amount of time you could be studying."

Dexter interjects. "That was a good, but I wouldn't just read it. You'll notice Todd uses his notes for reference and checks them as little as possible. You don't want to just read. It's not convincing enough."

I'm already exhausted. "Okay, I'll just concede then."

Dexter's eyes grow large. "*No*. Never, ever concede. It's an automatic loss, not only for you, but for our entire team."

I shake my head. "Sorry, I'm just drained. I don't think I can keep going."

"It's okay," says Dexter, "we can stop now. I just want to make sure you're ready because we're going to have a few more eyes on us this year."

"What do you mean?" I ask.

"They're going to be streaming the debate," Dexter says.

"On the Internet?"

"Yeah," says Dexter, nodding. "Isn't that cool?"

I don't like a lot of people watching me at one time, so I wouldn't describe it as *cool*.

***

As lunch approaches the next day, I start to worry. Nate is out sick and Perry has a dentist appointment, which means I'll have to do more talking if Reagan and Sophia join me. That'll cost me a lot of energy, so I'll need to limit my time in the cafeteria today. I feel tired enough as it is and have another debate practice in two days.

First, I plan to be late to lunch, which should waste a few minutes.

As the rest of the students head to the cafeteria, I stop at the water fountain to get a drink, and then *accidentally* spill a few drops on the ground. Of course, I wouldn't want anyone to slip, so I grab a towel from the bathroom and wipe it up.

I then walk down the hall and just before reaching my locker, turn and head back to my classroom.

"Did you forget something?" Ms. Walsh asks as I come back in.

"Yeah, my pencil."

I feel bad that I've interrupted Ms. Walsh. I'm pretty sure she's quiet too and I've just cut into her alone time.

She slides off her glasses. "I heard you made the debate team," she says. "Congratulations."

I look down, rubbing the corner of my eye. "Thanks …"

"You don't seem excited."

"No, it's fine. It's just … a lot of extra talking."

A small smile forms on her face. "Yeah, I get that," she says, "but just because it's a debate, doesn't mean you have to overdo it with the talking. Just be yourself."

"I don't know how that'll help."

"You'd be surprised," Ms. Walsh says.

I shrug, and then pick up the pencil I had left on purpose. After grabbing my lunch from my locker, I finally go to the cafeteria. As I head for my table, I notice Ronald sitting by himself. I stand there for a moment, holding my lunch, staring at him.

It's not fun to eat alone. That might sound strange coming from a quiet person, but it's true. Perry, Nate, and I don't talk much when we eat, but it's still nice having them there.

I cross through the cafeteria, weaving through students until I reach Ronald's table. He's hunched over a plate of pasta.

"Hi, Ronald," I say.

He tilts his head up, leaning away from me, his body tense. His shoulders relax when he recognizes me. "C—Colin ... right?

"Yeah," I say, nodding, then motion to the table. "Can I join you?"

Ronald pulls his tray back, making room. "Yeah, yeah, sure ..."

I sit down across from him and open my lunch. "Did you finish *Radioactive Jelly Beans*?" I ask.

He scoots forward, nodding rapidly, and his brown shirt rubs against the tomato sauce on his plate. "I j— just finished it. So good."

"Well don't tell me what happens because I'm only halfway through," I say.

"I—I won't," he says. "I promise."

I take a bite of my sandwich and we both sit in silence for a moment.

"You know the B—Botchaway brothers were wrong when they called you Master," he says.

"Really? Why?"

"When you address a boy, you're supposed to use master in front of his f—f—first name."

"Is that right?"

He nods. "They used it in f—front of your last name. It should be M—Master Colin Quigley, not Master Quigley."

I smile. "Thanks, I didn't know that."

"So uh ... uh ... w—what are you having for lunch?" he asks.

I turn my sandwich toward him. "Tuna fish."

"Oh, okay. And ... uh ... how do you like your classes?"

"They're good."

I know what Ronald's doing. He feels uncomfortable when no one's talking so he's trying to keep the conversation going.

"You know, Ronald, we don't have to talk if you don't want to. I'm perfectly fine just sitting here eating lunch with you."

A huge, crooked smile spreads across his face.

After a few minutes, a boy from my class, sitting at the end of the table, looks over. "What's wrong with you guys?" he asks. "Why are you being so quiet?"

Two-hundred and eighty-six.

"We're good," I say, chomping away on my sandwich. "We're just eating."

"Wait, are you Colin Quigley?" he asks.

"Yeah," I say.

"You're the one debating Reagan," he says.

I nod.

The boy turns to someone next him. "He's really doing it. Can you believe a quiet kid's going to debate Reagan?"

They both laugh.

I ignore them and continue eating. As I swallow down my last bite, I see Ronald's eyes fixed upon me.

"What?" I say.

"You're a really confident quiet person," he says.

I wipe my mouth with a napkin, lifting my shoulders. "I guess ..."

"I hate when someone calls me quiet." He sits back in his chair, his eyes still on me. "It doesn't seem to bother you. I don't know how you do it."

***

I lie in bed that evening reading *Radioactive Jelly Beans,* my first of three books for the reading challenge. My bed is my favorite place to read, with my head resting against a pillow. I prefer reading in my pajamas too, either before going to bed or when I wake up.

As I lie comfortably, with the bottom of the book resting against my chest, my door flies open.

"You're next, Colin!" Reagan says, pointing at me.

I gasp and drop my book. No one has ever barged into my room without knocking. "What ... what am I next for?"

"Your arm-wresting match. We're having a tournament."

"Who's in the tournament?" I ask.

"Your sister, the two of us, and your parents, whom I already beat."

I raise my eyebrows. "You beat my dad in arm-wresting?"

"Yeah, he was easier than your mom."

"But," I say, glancing down at my book, "I'm reading."

"Reading? Didn't you hear what I said? We're having an arm-wrestling tournament. We do this all the time in Texas."

I glance around my room, then out the window. "But we're not in Texas."

She extends her arms wide. "Well I'm bringing Texas to you."

"Can you arm-wrestle Violet first? I'd like to finish this chapter."

Reagan shakes her head. "Your sister ran out of the house when I asked her. She's lucky I didn't call that a forfeit."

I sigh and push my book aside. "Okay, fine."

She drops to her stomach, sets her elbow down, and then raises her forearm.

"We're doing this on the floor?" I ask. "I haven't vacuumed this week."

"You vacuum?" she asks.

I lean up in bed. "Yes, once a week. Every Saturday."

Reagan shakes her head and groans. "You're the only boy I know that vacuums. You should be fixing vacuums, not using them." She waves me over. "Your carpet's fine, come on."

I slide off my bed and lie down on the floor, facing her. I can feel her breath against my face. There's no need to ask her what she had for lunch, I'm certain it was a peanut butter sandwich.

"Who's your favorite arm-wrestler?" she asks.

"My favorite arm-wrestler?" I say, lifting my shoulders. "I don't know any arm—"

"Mine is John Brzenk," she says, cutting me off. "He's the best. I can't wait to go against him. I plan to start arm-wrestling professionally when I turn eighteen." She flexes her hand. "What's your best technique?"

"I've never arm-wrestled, so I don't know any techniques … except just to push your arm down."

"Mine is the top-roll, although I used the hook on your mom." Reagan slides her arm toward me. "Okay, let's do this."

I grab hold of her sweaty hand and dig my elbow into the carpet. Dust flies up and I wave it away. I do need to vacuum.

"On three," she says.

I squeeze her hand tighter. I am going to destroy her. No one gets away with interrupting my reading, and no one makes fun of my vacuuming.

She begins to count down. "One ..."

My eyes narrow.

"Two ..."

I clench my teeth.

"Three!"

Reagan drives my arm into the floor in less than a second. She hops to her feet as I roll onto my back, grimacing in pain.

"I'm going to go beat your mom and dad again," she says. "I'll be back in twenty minutes for round two."

I clutch my throbbing wrist. "Can you bring ice?"

***

That weekend, I decide to stop by Nate's house to see how he's feeling.

"Hello," Nate says, greeting me at the door.

His voice is flat and his face pale, but that's typical for Nate.

"I thought you had a cold," I say.

"Oh right ... cough, cough," Nate says, holding his hand to his mouth.

"So you're not sick?" I ask.

"Define sick," he says.

I laugh, glancing past him. "Is Dexter home?"

"No."

"What about the rest of your family?"

"No."

"Where did they go?"

"Out to eat."

"And they didn't take you?"

"No, because I'm still, you know, cough, cough, sick."

With Nate's cold having been miraculously cured, I decide to stay.

He shows me the three books he bought for the reading challenge, spreading them on the table. "*Probability and Statistics for Engineering and the Sciences, Informed Decisions using Data*, and *Naked Statistics*."

Nate pauses and takes a couple breaths.

"It's okay," I say, "It was a long sentence."

He waits a moment, then speaks again. "But Naked Statistics isn't like ... about ..."

"I didn't think it was," I say.

Nate taps one of the books. "I've finished *Probability and Statistics for Engineering and the*

Sciences, and I've completed seventy-two percent of *Informed Decisions using Data*."

He blows out a mouthful of air.

"Just use *book one*, *book two*, and *book three*," I say. "It'll save you some words."

Nate nods. "How many books have you finished? We should try to stay in sync."

I shake my head. "Sorry, I'm still on my first."

BEEP. BEEP. BEEP.

Nate taps a button on his watch.

"What was that?" I ask.

"The alarm on my watch."

"I know, but what was it for?"

"It's the approximate time I thought my family would be home, minus one minute."

I glance at his watch. "Why minus one minute?"

"So I would have time to return to my bed and pretend to be sleeping."

"Because you're still... cough, cough, sick?" I ask.

"Yes."

We hear a car door close. Nate closes his eyes and puts a hand over his face.

"What's wrong," I ask?

"I didn't factor in that you'd be here."

"What does that mean?" I ask.

"It means I won't have time to get you out before they come in," Nate says. "And when they see you here, they'll assume I'm better."

Dexter walks through the door a few seconds later, followed by Nate's parents.

"You're up!" Dexter says to Nate. "You must be feeling better."

Nate groans, his hand still covering his face.

"Hey, Colin," Dexter says. "Is Nate showing you his books for the reading challenge? I'll tell you, he's determined to finish. Every time I try to talk to him now, his face goes right into one of those books." He sits down in the chair next to me. "So listen, I've been thinking about the debate. I wonder if we should have you practice against someone quiet. You know, to help build your confidence and get you going."

I point to Nate. "I could debate Nate ... or Perry. I mean, I know some quiet kids."

Dexter nods. "I figured you would. Can you bring a few of your friends to the next debate practice?"

"Sure," I say.

"Okay, now here's my next thought," he says. "During your preparation time, I'd consider writing your notes on index cards. Writing everything on a single sheet of paper hasn't been working that well for you. The index cards will keep you better organized."

Dexter's debating advice continues for the next ten minutes, and although his suggestions are helpful, I've reached my limit. Nothing else is going to fit into my brain. I need to get out of here.

I watch his mouth, waiting for him to suck in a breath. It'll be my best chance to escape.

"I'd also try listening to what the other debater is saying, and not just have a prepared speech," Dexter continues. "You'd be surprised how many people don't actually *listen* to what their opponent is saying."

Come on, inhale already.

"And then it's just a matter of taking what you've learned during your preparation time, and working that into your argument."

Then I hear the air go in and see his chest rise.

I leap out of my seat and shoot for the door. "Sorry, I'm late for dinner!"

"Bye Nate! Bye Dexter!"

I'm out the door before Dexter lets out a breath.

CHAPTER 6

TACO TUESDAY

With the debate two weeks away, Dexter has us practice in the auditorium where the actual debate will be held. He says the sessions with Todd have been helping, but he wants me to get comfortable debating in a larger room. And as he suggested, I've brought Nate and Perry with me.

We step onto the stage and our footsteps echo through the room as we approach Dexter and Todd.

"Hey guys," says Dexter, leaning up from the podium. "Are you ready to debate?"

We all look at each other, and then nod.

"Oh … *yes*," I say, and then turn to my friends. "In a debate, you're supposed to say 'yes' and 'no' instead of nodding or shaking your head."

"But we're not in a debate yet," says Nate.

Dexter smiles. "That's true, Nate, but I'd suggest using debate techniques even if you're not officially debating. It helps build self-confidence."

"What if I don't want to build self-confidence?" says Nate.

Todd claps his hands together. "How about we get started."

Dexter and Todd pick Nate as my first opponent. He gives us our topic and lets us research it for twenty minutes. When we're done, they have us stand at the podiums and give us advice on posturing, facial expressions, and gestures.

After Dexter, Todd, and Perry take their seats in the first row of the auditorium, I remain at the podium, organizing my index cards. Then I peek over at Nate, who isn't organizing anything. Although he did research the topic, Nate didn't take any notes. He does the same thing in class.

"Let's begin," says Dexter. "Again, the topic is 'school should be year round for students in grades one through twelve.' Nate will argue for, Colin will argue against. Todd, Perry, and I will judge the debate, and I'll serve as moderator."

Nate raises his hand.

"Yes?" says Dexter.

"Why is Perry wearing sunglasses?"

We all look at Perry, who now has on large, round sunglasses.

"That's how TV judges roll these days," says Perry, crossing his legs.

Todd shakes his head. "Can we please start?"

"Yes," says Dexter, and then points to Nate. "You're up, brother."

"School should be year-round," says Nate.

A long moment goes by as we wait for him to continue.

"So … is that your initial argument?" asks Dexter.

"Yes," says Nate.

Todd rubs the side of his head. "You just repeated the topic."

"Yes," says Nate.

It's time for me to counter. I straighten my body and clear my throat. "Research has shown that students who attend year-round schools have the exact same performance as students who attend schools with summer breaks." I pause, remembering Dexter's advice about making eye contact.

My eyes move from Nate to Dexter to Todd, and then to Perry. Of course, I can't see Perry's eyes because he's wearing sunglasses.

"Plus, part of a student's learning experience comes from things *outside* the classroom," I say. "Think of all the skills you've learned at summer camp, and all the knowledge you've gained from reading books and watching television. But not like reality television, more like the National Geographic channel …although I think they have reality shows now too."

Dexter gives me a thumbs-up, then turns his head to Nate.

"Nate, is there anything you'd like to add to your argument?" says Dexter. "Maybe like what percentage of knowledge gained during the school year is lost in the summer."

"It's fifty-three percent," says Nate.

"That's good," says Dexter. "So fifty-three percent of what a student learns during the year is lost over the summer?"

"Yes," says Nate.

Todd covers his eyes.

"Okay," says Dexter. He motions to Todd and Perry. "I'll consult with the judges now."

They lean their heads together and begin whispering. I peek over at Nate, whose expression hasn't changed. He's staring straight ahead, no emotion on his face.

"Well, this was a close one," says Dexter, "but we felt Colin's argument had a little more … *substance* to it, so we're declaring him the winner."

I lift my chin and push out my chest, looking confidently at the judges. It's my first debate win, against an extremely tough opponent.

"Todd, Perry, anything else to add," says Dexter.

"That was the worse debate I've ever seen," says Todd.

Perry adjusts his sunglasses. "Yeah, I could hear Nate's same argument at any karaoke bar. I didn't care for it." He tilts his head down and looks at me over his sunglasses. "Now, I thought Colin was *okay* … but I wish I would have seen a little more movement from him. He was a bit stiff."

Next up is Perry, and I'm not crazy about the topic. It's 'Aliens exist.' Dexter wanted to use a topic Perry was familiar with to make the debate more challenging for me.

Perry joins me on stage and we begin our research, although I'm sure Perry knows plenty already. The first debate has dwindled my talk capacity though and I'm having trouble concentrating.

After twenty minutes, Perry and I take our places at the podiums, but I only have a few notes written down and little energy.

"Okay, Perry, you're arguing for Aliens existing and Colin is arguing against," says Dexter. "Please begin."

"Most experts agree that there are over one-hundred million galaxies in the universe," says Perry.

"One-hundred billion," says Nate.

Perry tilts the podium microphone toward him. "Did I say a million?" says Perry.

"Yes," says Nate.

"Sorry, I'm a little nervous," says Perry.

Todd glares at Nate. "Judges aren't allowed to interact with the debaters."

"Okay," says Nate, looking straight ahead.

"Please proceed, Perry," says Dexter.

"So if there are over one-hundred billion galaxies in the universe, and if each galaxy has two-hundred and fifty trillion planets like ours does, then that would work out to …" Perry says, eyeing Nate.

"I'm not allowed to respond," says Nate. "Although technically I just did."

"Like a zillion planets," says Perry. "And if there are a zillion planets out there, the chances are high that one of them would support life."

I feel Dexter and Todd's eyes turn to me, waiting for my counter. "Uh …" I say, shuffling through my notes. "Not all of the … uh … two-hundred and fifty trillion planets in our galaxy can support life, so it wouldn't be a zillion."

"That's true," says Perry, "but there's fifty billion that can, so that works out to, I don't know, a half a zillion."

I try to say something, but the only thing that comes out is a yawn.

"Would you like to take a nap, Colin?" asks Todd.

"I didn't think judges were allowed to interact with the debaters," says Nate.

Dexter places his index finger against his lips. "Let them continue please."

"And consider the fact that there are thousands of unexplained sightings each year," says Perry.

My mind is groggy and I can fccl the weight of my eyelids pressing down. "But there's no like … proof," I say.

"There have been hundreds of documented cases of alien abductions," says Perry.

I fight back another yawn and scan my notes, but before I can organize a thought, I hear Perry again. He goes on for five minutes and I'm unable to respond even once. Dexter gives me time for a rebuttal, but I've got nothing.

After huddling with Todd and Nate, Dexter announces the winner.

"Well, we thought you both did very well, but we felt one of you had more passion and provided more detail in your argument. So …"

"Perry won," says Nate.

"Well, let's provide constructive feedback," says Dexter.

"Perry did better," says Nate.

Dexter tries to encourage me, but Nate's right. Perry did better, much better. I realize Perry knows more about the topic, but if I can't beat a quiet kid in a debate after practicing for two weeks, how will I ever beat Reagan?

***

As I sit down at the kitchen table, my dad slides a plate in front of me. I stare at the two tacos resting against each other.

"Wait, what is this?" I ask. "It's Saturday. We should be having fish and chips."

"Reagan wanted tacos tonight," Dad says, scooting his chair in.

"But we do tacos on Tuesday. You know, *taco Tuesday*."

Reagan shakes her head. "Your weird little eating schedule was driving me bananas, so we're doing tacos on Saturday this week."

"But that doesn't make sense," I say.

Reagan bites into her taco. "Why not?"

"Because Saturday doesn't start with a T."

"Why does the day have to start with a T?"

"Because that's how it goes. *T*—aco *T*—uesday."

Reagan reaches her hand into the lettuce bowl, pushes the spoon aside, and grabs a handful. She jams it into her taco. "That's ridiculous."

"We'll get back to our regular schedule next week," my mom says.

"Fine," I say, and then notice that my knife, fork and spoon are missing. "Wait, where are my utensils?"

"You don't need utensils for tacos," says Reagan. She leans over the table, talking to me like I'm a baby. "But I put a napkin right next to your plate, just the way you like it."

I move the napkin from the right side of the plate to the left. "It's on the wrong side though," I say under my breath.

"Hey, Mr. Q, since I set the table tonight, can I get that limited edition Joe Mufferaw book? You know, as a reward."

My dad shakes his head.

"What if I clean up after dinner?"

My dad shakes his head again.

"Did I tell you he was my favorite lumberjack?"

My dad nods.

As I reach for the salad tongs to begin adding my toppings, I see drippings from Reagan's hand on the lettuce. So much for greens in my tacos. And just as I go for the cheese, Reagan's hand plunges into it, grabbing half a bowl's worth. So much for anything in my tacos.

Then Reagan starts babbling on about how the tacos in Texas are so much better than the ones in Virginia. I feel bad for my dad because it's his day to cook and Reagan is tearing apart his tacos. But there's not much he could have changed. He used a kit, and as he always does, as all quiet people do, he followed the instructions exactly.

"So what makes your tacos so much better?" I ask.

"Well, Texas is close to South America, and South Americans know how to make better tacos."

"I think she's talking about restaurant tacos," my mom says. "Right, Reagan?"

"No, we use a kit."

"Which kit?" I ask.

"Old El Paso."

I sit up in my chair. "You're kidding."

"No," she says. "I love Old El Paso."

"That's the kit my dad used."

Using the back of her hand, she wipes taco sauce from her mouth. "So what?"

"So how can your tacos be better if we're both using the same kit?"

"I guess my parents just make them better."

"But it's the exact same kit. It's the same ingredients, the same instructions."

"Maybe he missed a step."

I hold up a finger, my voice rising. "I guarantee my father didn't miss a step. Right, Dad?"

"Right," my father says, and then goes back to eating his taco.

"No offense, Mr. Q. I just like my parents' tacos better."

My father holds up his hand, indicating no hard feelings.

"I'm excited to watch the two of you debate?" my mother says.

I set down my taco. "You know about the debate?"

"Yes, Mrs. Connolly told me," she says.

"How did she find out?" I ask.

"Mrs. Wilson told her," she says. "We had quite the discussion about it during book club."

I turn my palms up. "I thought you were supposed to discuss books at book club?"

"It's not a rule, Colin," says Reagan. "They can talk about whatever they want, even about how I'm going to obliterate you in the debate."

I've just about had it with Reagan. She's loud, cocky, inconsiderate, and tries to control every conversation. I need to take a verbal-stand.

But I'm tired, so if I'm going to attempt this tonight, I'll need a boost. It's time, I decide. It's time for a soda. They seem to make Perry more talkative so maybe they'll do the same for me.

My mom obliges and pours me my first soda. I try it. It's sweet, kind of like liquid-cake. It gives me a sudden surge of energy, and out of nowhere a strange thought comes to me.

"I wonder why you have to peel certain fruits," I say.

"Say what?" Reagan says with half a taco in her mouth.

"Well, you have to peel fruits like oranges and bananas, but you don't have to peel apples or grapes."

Reagan keeps chewing as she talks. "The peel keeps the fruit fresh."

"I'm not debating whether the peel keeps it fresh because it's possible to peel an apple or even a grape. I'm just wondering why I have to peel a banana."

"You peel it, Colin, because you can't eat the skin."

"But how do you know? Have you ever eaten a banana peel?"

Reagan's face scrunches up into a confused look. "Why would I eat a banana peel?"

"No, the question is, why *wouldn't* you eat a banana peel? It might be delicious."

"It's not delicious, it's a banana peel. It's disgusting."

"But how do you know? Maybe we've been doing it wrong all these years. Maybe banana peels are better than cookies." I look over at the bananas on the counter. "I think I'm going to have a banana peel for dessert tonight."

Reagan shakes her head. "That's the stupidest thing I've ever heard."

My eyes grow large. "The stupidest or the most *genius*?"

"The stupidest, definitely the stupidest. What's wrong with you tonight? You better not eat tacos before the debate."

I ignore her, take another giant gulp of soda, and something else pops into my head.

"You know what would be a great pizza topping," I say. "*Pizza*."

She leans closer. "Say what?"

"They should make a pizza with smaller pizzas as the topping."

"But that's just one pizza on top of another pizza," Reagan says.

"No, the smaller pizzas on top would be the topping. They'd just have to make them really small, like the size of pepperoni."

She shakes her head. "That's absurd. No one's going to order a pizza with other pizzas as the topping."

"Sure they would, it would be so cool." I give my best pizza-ordering impression, holding a pretend-phone up to my ear. "Yes, I'd like to order a large pizza, half pepperoni, half pizza."

"No, what would be cool is making a taco that doesn't fall apart when you eat it," she says. "Again, no offense, Mr. Q, but your tacos are a little flimsy."

"No they're not," I say. "And how could you make a taco that doesn't fall apart? It's not possible."

"Sure it is. You could just make them bite-size so the entire taco could fit in your mouth. That way it wouldn't fall apart on your plate."

That's not a bad idea.

"That's a terrible idea," I say. "Why would someone eat fifty tiny tacos when they could just eat three regular ones?"

"So they wouldn't fall apart, that's why. Plus, how cool would it be to say, 'I ate fifty tacos!'"

That would be pretty cool.

"And I know what I'm talking about because I'm part South American," she says.

I look her up and down. "But South America is a continent, it's not like a nationality."

She shakes her head. "I don't know about that, I think Texans are considered South Americans. I mean South America is right on the border."

"Actually, Mexico's on the border ... and I think Mexico is considered part of North America."

"But Mexico's really short," she says. "South

America is like right there. I think I hit it with a rock once."

My energy level is dropping. I can't keep up with her. I'm about to ask for another soda, but I stop myself. It's useless. I would need a hundred sodas to keep up with Reagan.

I finish my taco and go to my room.

***

When I wake up the next morning, my head is throbbing. I suspect it's from the soda last night. It sure made me feel good at the time, but I'm paying for it today.

Rolling onto my side, I notice the book *Radioactive Jelly Beans* on my nightstand. I still haven't finished it because *someone* keeps interrupting me, and since I'm certain it's going to happen again, I don't bother picking it up. Nate's already on his third book for the reading challenge and I haven't even finished one.

Perry and Nate both call, but I ask my mom to take messages. It's the third time I've ignored their calls this week, but I don't have the energy to talk, not even to my friends.

I skip my usual bowl of Rice Krispies and slip out the back door. After scooping up a few soccer balls, I head to the back of my yard where my soccer goal is set up. I'm hoping a little physical activity will make me feel better.

As I approach the goal, I see Larry and Stanley Botchaway, who are sitting on their patio, books in hand. It's at least eighty degrees, but they're wearing their usual long pants and collared shirts.

I set down the soccer balls. Pretending this is the championship game, I fire shots past an imaginary goalkeeper, raising my hands after each winning kick.

Then the backdoor flies open and Reagan tears into the yard. "I'm ready." She strides past me and plants herself in the goal.

"What are you doing?" I ask.

"What does it look like I'm doing? I'm playing soccer."

"So ... you want me to shoot on you?"

"Well, I saw you from the window and I wouldn't call what you're doing shooting, but sure."

I roll my eyes. But as I stand there with my foot on the ball, a smile creeps across my face. I get to kick something at Reagan and I won't even get in trouble for it. What a great way to start the day. My head is feeling better already.

"I have to warn you," I say. "I can kick the ball pretty hard."

"If you say so," she says.

I take a step back, and then fire a shot right at her. Reagan swats at it, knocking the ball away with one hand.

"You kick like a girl," she says.

"What?"

"I said you kick like a girl."

"But ... isn't that an insult to you, since you're a girl."

She takes a step forward. "I don't kick like a girl!"

I shake my head and line up for another shot. "Tell me if *this* feels like a girl's shot." I fire the next shot, low and to the right corner. She swings her leg out and knocks the ball to the side. "Yup, still like a girl."

As I set down another ball, I notice Violet come through the backdoor and onto the deck. Upon seeing Reagan, Violet's mouth falls open, as if a herd of buffalo is charging toward her. She begins to backpedal into the house, but Reagan spots her.

"Hey!" says Reagan, walking toward her. "We still need to arm-wrestle!"

Violet screams, jumps back inside, and slams the door shut.

Reagan returns to the goal and waves at me to take another shot. I hit it hard, but miss by three feet.

She yawns. "Okay, are you done warming up? When are you going to start shooting for real?"

"How about now?"

I move back ten feet, then exhale. I'm going kick this ball harder than I've kicked any ball in my entire life. I grit my teeth, charge toward the ball, and blast it at the top left corner. Reagan leaps and tips it over the goal. She stops my next twenty shots, two with her face. I think she blocked one just with her mouth.

After slapping away another shot, she smirks, standing with her hands on her hips. "Just like Joe Mufferaw."

"I thought he was a lumberjack," I say.

"He was a lumberjack, but he was awesome at everything ... including being able to stop girly soccer shots."

Frustrated, I kick a soccer ball and it slams against our metal shed.

Larry Botchaway slams his book closed. "Can you *please* keep it down."

I hold up a hand. "Sorry."

"Perhaps you can miskick your soccer ball at the local park," Larry says.

"I like playing in my backyard," I say.

Larry holds up his book. "Well, I like to read in my backyard and you're interrupting me."

"*Sorry.* I usually read in my room."

"May I ask what you're reading?" says Stanley.

"*Radioactive Jelly Beans,*" I say.

Larry and Stanley exchange glances.

"Reagan, I'm afraid they haven't lined up a worthy debate opponent for you," says Larry.

"I know," says Reagan, nodding. "But don't worry, I still plan to dominate."

I press my lips together. "I'm not going to lose the debate just because I'm reading *Radioactive Jelly Beans.*"

Stanley chuckles. "As if that were the only reason."

"Here's what you should be reading," says Larry. He turns the cover of his book toward me. "*The Great Gatsby.* By F. Scott Fitzgerald."

I shake my head. "I haven't read it."

"I'm shocked," says Stanley.

"So what made this dude so great?" I ask.

"Well for starters," says Larry, "he didn't waste his time reading children's science fiction books."

Reagan giggles.

I scratch my head and stare at Larry. "That really wouldn't make him great."

"He also didn't spend time winning pretend soccer games in his backyard," says Larry.

"Do you really do that?" Reagan says, holding her hand over her mouth, still giggling.

I glare at her.

"Nor did he play video games for four consecutive hours every Saturday afternoon," says Larry.

Reagan clutches her stomach and begins laughing out loud. "I *know* you do that!"

"It's every Saturday morning," I say. "Saturday afternoon is when I vacuum."

"Gatsby also didn't try to get by on thirty-nine words a day," says Larry.

I cross my arms against my chest. "What is that supposed to mean?"

Larry turns his nose up. "And he wasn't a weirdo."

My face turns red. "I'm not a weirdo!"

Reagan bends over at the waist, howling, her mouth stretched open. She looks like a monster. She *looks* like an alien. Maybe Perry's right, maybe Reagan is an alien. And maybe, just maybe, water will destroy her.

As Reagan continues laughing, I walk to the house and grab the garden hose by the nozzle. The hose unravels as I walk toward her. Then I stop. What if she is an alien? If water changes Reagan into her true alien form, I'll need a weapon to protect myself.

I spot my nerf-gun on the deck and hurry over to it. I grab it, and then begin to sneak up on her, the hose in one hand and the nerf-gun in the other. She has her back to me as I reach her.

I'm ready. I'm ready to attack the talking-alien.

Reagan peeks over her shoulder and sees me. I panic and squeeze the nozzle. Water shoots out, drenching her from her spiky black hair all the way down to her oversized sneakers. She wipes the water from her eyes and glares at me.

I drop the hose and aim the nerf-gun at her.

Her mouth opens. "What are you doing!"

Here it comes ... she's about to change into an alien.

She moves closer. "Why did you squirt me!"

Any second now ...

"Colin! What is wrong with you?"

Oops.

I guess she's not an alien after all, or at least not one I can destroy with water.

"Uh ... sorry, Reagan, I was trying to water the petunias."

She points at the flowers, water still dripping from her arm. "They're twenty feet behind you!"

"Oh ... yeah ... sorry. I missed."

I look over and see Larry and Stanley staring at me, their mouths hanging open.

Larry's eyes move to my left hand. "Master Quigley, why are you pointing a nerf-gun at her?"

My parents ground me for two days. I've only been grounded once before, and that time I was restricted from playing video games and going outside. Honestly, it wasn't that bad of a punishment. I spent my time reading and vacuuming, so it was actually kind of nice.

But this punishment doesn't go so well. Instead of restricting me from certain activities or confining me to my room, my parents make me play with Reagan. They know me too well, because this punishment is absolute torture.

CHAPTER 7

THE BRICK WALL

Staring out the window in class the next day, I notice myself in the reflection. I look pale and have huge circles under my eyes. And that's just my appearance. I feel worse. I feel like I've caught a bug— a loud, obnoxious bug that never, ever stops talking— and I have to out-debate her in less than two weeks.

Then I notice students looking over at me every few minutes, whispering and pointing. I'm not used to this much attention.

"You're Colin, right?" a girl next to me whispers.

"Yeah."

"I'm quiet too," she says.

I give her a thumbs-up.

"And so is my mom," she says. "It would mean a lot to us if you won."

I gulp. "I'll try ..."

Then I hear a boy snickering behind her. "A quiet kid can't beat a loud kid in a debate," he says. "It's impossible."

She shakes her head. "It's not impossible."

"It is," the boy says. "He's going to get destroyed. I even bet my quiet little sister twenty bucks."

"Well, I think Colin can do it," the girl says to him, "and so do other quiet kids."

The boy smirks. "How would you know? You're all quiet. You never talk to each other."

The girl waves a finger. "Don't listen to him, Colin. We're all rooting for you and we're all going to come watch you in the debate."

"I'm going to watch him, too," says the boy, laughing. "Watch him get slaughtered."

***

After class, on my way to the cafeteria, I see Sophia walking in the opposite direction. Although I'm in no mood for a conversation, I am happy to see her. Based on Reagan's prediction about her lifeline, there was a chance she could have died last Thursday. She's about a week past that, so I think she'll be okay. I guess a person's lifeline isn't too accurate after all, at least not for girls.

I wave to her as she passes me. She looks worn out.

"Is everything okay?" I ask.

"Yeah, everything's fine," she says, slowing down briefly. "I just forgot to do my history homework. I'm going to skip lunch so I can finish it before class."

She gives me a weak smile and moves down the hall. I continue toward the cafeteria, and then suddenly stop.

Wait a second. Skipping lunch to do homework? That sure sounds familiar.

A bit suspicious, I leave lunch a few minutes early and head to Mr. Melacki's classroom. I stop at the door and peek inside. Sophia is sitting in her desk, one hand propped up against her cheek, her eyes half open. She's not doing homework at all, she's resting.

Later that day, on the bus ride home, I watch Sophia. Luckily I can do this in peace since Reagan is sitting with the popular girls. Sophia is chatting with a girl next to her. I must be imagining things because she looks like her normal talkative self.

A minute later, after the bus stops and the girl next to her hops off, Sophia exhales and closes her eyes. The bus pulls away and immediately Sophia's head begins jerking up and down. She's having trouble staying awake. The conversation has drained her.

Well, what do you know? The loud girl is actually quiet.

***

As I lie in bed that night, I think about Sophia. I've seen her type before.

There are two types of quiet people. The first type is quiet and simply accepts it, like me. The second type is secretly quiet. They go well above their talk-capacity so they appear loud and carefree, even though that's not their true personality. They do this because they're afraid of being labeled a quiet person.

Looking back, the signs were there: she packs her lunch, she likes to read, she sits by herself on the bus, and she enjoys hanging out with quiet kids. This is classic quiet kid behavior. I can't believe I never saw it. I laugh as I think back to the fire drill. Sophia wasn't being quiet to win the bet; she wanted to stop talking so she could regain her energy. How sneaky.

The next morning, Sophia boards the bus and takes her usual seat, a few rows in front of mine.

"Hi, Sophia," I say with a smirk.

She turns back to me. "Hey, Colin."

I study her face. She's trying to look cheerful and carefree, but I know better. To be sure about my theory though, I decide to perform one final test.

"Do you want to hear a funny story?" I ask her.

She sucks in a breath. "Okay."

"It's a long story, are you sure?"

Sophia pauses. "Yeah, yeah … I'm sure."

Her shoulders slump and she begins rubbing her temples. She's preparing herself, preparing to have her listening-capacity drained. I know this look well.

I just smile at her.

"Why are you looking at me like that?" she says. "I thought you were going to tell me a funny story."

"I know your secret."

"What? What secret?"

"You're quiet."

A look of terror fills Sophia's face and her cheeks turn pink. Her eyes shift to the front of the bus.

"Don't worry, I won't tell anyone," I say.

"I'm sorry, Colin, I don't know what you're talking about," she says, her voice low.

I hold her gaze. "Yes you do. You're quiet."

She crosses her arms over her chest. "No I'm not."

"Yes you are. I know a quiet person when I see one and you're quiet."

"Well if that were true, why didn't you say anything before?"

I scoot closer, letting my arms hang over the seat in front of me. "Because I just found out. I have to give you credit, you hide it pretty well."

Sophia looks down for a moment, hesitating. "Okay, okay," she says, her voice still low. "I'm a quarter quiet."

"A *quarter* quiet?"

She blows out a breath. "Yes. My grandfather on my mother's side was quiet."

"So you're not like a hundred percent quiet?"

"Right. My mom's fifty percent and I'm twenty-five percent. I can talk a lot more than you, Perry, and Nate, but not as much as a regular person." She glances toward the front of the bus again, then back to me. "So how much do you want?"

"For what?"

"To not tell anyone I'm a quarter quiet. Five dollars? Ten?"

"Uh … you don't have to pay me. I think it's neat that you're a quarter quiet. I'm not going to tell anyone."

"You think it's *neat*?"

"Yeah, you should be proud that you're a quarter quiet. It's really cool."

Her mouth curves into a small smile. "I think you're really cool, Colin."

This time my face turns pink, and I look down.

"I don't know how you do it," she says. "Everyone calling you quiet all the time."

I glance up at her. "It really doesn't bother me."

"I don't think I could handle it."

"Why?"

She lifts her shoulders. "I'd be afraid that everyone would think I'm … weird."

I nod, hesitating. "Do you think I'm weird?"

Sophia shakes her head. "No, not at all."

"Then you shouldn't feel weird either," I say. "Plus, there are lots of perks."

"Like what?"

"Better listening skills, greater attention to detail, higher grades … the list goes on and on." I sink back into my seat and stare out the window. "You know what's funny though?"

"What?" she asks.

"I don't get tired when I talk to you. Talking to everyone else exhausts me, but not you. I don't get it."

***

At home on Tuesday evening, I settle into my reading spot on my bed. Dexter lent me a book on debate strategies that I want to get started on.

Reagan reads at the kitchen table, and even does her homework there. The kitchen is the busiest room in the house, so I don't know how she's able to get anything done. Maybe that's why her answers in class are so ridiculous. She's probably combining real facts with random conversations. The only way I can read and remember anything is if I'm alone in my room. If I hear one person talking, it's over.

After finishing the first two chapters, I decide to go downstairs and watch debate videos on the computer. But I'm worried that Reagan will see me, so I'm going to need to do this quietly. I think I can handle it. I have a lot of experience being quiet.

Cracking my door open, I peer out into the hallway. It's clear. I slip out of my room and step lightly down the stairs, skipping the fourth step, which is the creaky one. Reagan is flipping through a textbook at the kitchen table, turning to my mom every few seconds to say something. My mom looks exhausted.

As if my socks were snow skis, I slide past the kitchen along the hardwood floors. I feel like a cross-country skier as I coast down the hallway. I bank left, glide into my Dad's office, and find my sister is at the computer typing an email.

"Hey, Violet, can I use the computer?"

She nods and holds up a finger. She does this a lot. It's an easy way for her to communicate without having to talk. A minute later, Violet gets up and leaves the office.

My sister uses email quite a bit, a ton more than she uses the telephone. For her, talking on the telephone is much more draining. She could write a thousand emails and not be as tired as if she made a single telephone call.

I must say, email has been a huge win for the quiet community. Before email, the way people communicated, except for the occasional hand written letter, was face to face or by telephone. Both of those require talking. With email, there is no talking. What could be better than that? Talk about an energy saver! Many people think that Alexander Graham Bell's invention of the telephone is the most significant communication invention in history. I disagree. It's definitely email.

Unfortunately, I can't take advantage of email until I get my own email address, which my parents won't allow until I turn thirteen. Most kids look forward to sixteen when they can start driving. Not me. I look forward to thirteen when I can start emailing.

As I settle into my dad's chair, I notice my sister has Facebook up, which is another great tool for quiet people. It's a website that allows its members to post stuff on the Internet, like things they've done and places they've been. So when someone asks my sister what she's been up to, she just points them to her Facebook page. How easy is that? No talking required.

Still, I'm not so sure I'll join. I think I'd get tired of reading about *other* people's activities. I've seen my sister's friends post things like 'I just ate four hotdogs' and 'I just went to the gym.' Who cares? And why did they feel the need to share these things with all of their friends? Now if someone posted something about reaching the summit of Mount Everest, okay then, that would be a worthy post; but just about everything else is ridiculous. I don't care that Kate hates her new haircut, I don't care that Billy came in fourth in his swim meet, and I especially don't care that Carly has checked-in at Dunkin Donuts.

As I scarch the Internet for debate videos, I hear footsteps thumping down the hall. Then I hear that squeaky voice.

"What are you doing?" Reagan asks, coming into the office. "I'm done with my homework."

How does she keep finding me? She should work

for the missing persons department. Of course, she would only find quiet kids, but still.

And I despise that verbal combination: a question, followed by an unrelated statement. Not that I wanted to answer her first question, but it would have been polite to allow it.

She leans over me, squinting at the computer. "Seven principles of good debating," she says, reading the screen. "You can't study for a debate. The topics are random."

"I know, Reagan. I'm not studying for it. I'm just learning some new techniques."

Reagan licks her fingers, which are covered in powder. "It's not going to matter."

"What's on your fingers?" I ask.

"It's from the donuts," she says.

My eyes widen. "The donuts that were on the counter?"

"Yeah."

"Those are for Sunday."

"Why Sunday?" she asks, continuing to suck off the powder, one finger at a time.

"Because that's when we eat donuts. It's our weekly breakfast treat, once a week, every Sunday morning."

She licks her lips. "You're going to have to skip this week."

I may need to go to Dunkin Donuts. I wonder if I'll see Carly there.

From the reflection in the monitor, I see Violet step back into the office. She must have forgotten something. But as soon as Violet spots the back of Reagan's head, she leaves the room.

Reagan points at the computer. "Look, you're not going to learn how to debate by watching videos on a computer. If you want to learn how to debate, than just debate." With her thumb, she motions for me to stand. "Up, up, up. I'm going to find a debate topic for us."

"Why?"

"Because we're going to debate."

"Against each other?" I ask. "You're on the other team."

"You're my cousin, so I'm going to help you out. You're never going to beat me, but if you practice enough maybe the elementary school debate team will take you."

I let out a breath and rise from the chair.

Reagan plops down, grabs the mouse, and begins typing on the keyboard, coating both with white donut powder.

I slide a chair over and sit down next to her.

"Okay, here we go," she says. "Schools should allow junk food in vending machines." She turns her chair and faces me. "I'll argue for, you argue against. Ready—go."

"Wo, wo, wo," I say. "I need to prepare. We're supposed to have twenty minutes."

Reagan laughs. "Just start debating. I never prepare."

"You don't use the twenty minutes?" I ask.

"Never," she says. "When I practice with Larry and Stanley, I do push-ups during the preparation time."

"But ... I need time to research the topic. I can't just start talking about it."

She slides her chair closer, looking me in the eye. "I'm going to start this debate in three seconds. When I do, I want you to debate me. No preparation. Just debate me. I'll start with the pro, then you counter."

My heart begins to pound.

She scoots her chair back and sits up straight. "One ... two ... three."

"I'm given the right to eat junk food by the Constitution of the United States of America," Reagan says. "If we give up the right to eat junk food, we give

141

up our freedom, and an America without freedom is a freedom-less America."

I stare at her, my heart still pounding.

"Now you want to counter," she says.

"But …"

"Come on," she says.

"Uh …"

"*Counter*, Colin."

"I don't know what to say."

"*Counter*!"

"Errr …"

She stands from her chair. "I said counter, Colin!!!"

I rise. "Your argument isn't valid! The constitution doesn't stop you from eating junk food! The school can serve whatever it wants! If you choose to bring junk food to school and eat it, than fine, you can do that! But the school doesn't have to serve it in the vending machines on its property!"

I collapse into my chair.

"That wasn't half bad," she says, staring down at me. "Let's do another one."

Breathing heavily, I wave her off. "I can't."

"Why?"

"It took too much out of me."

She glances at the clock on the wall. "But that was like forty seconds. How are you going to last for an entire debate?"

"I don't know ..."

"And you do realize we're debating three separate topics, right?"

My shoulders slump. "Yes."

I rub the side of my head as pain builds behind my eyes. I need a serious people-break. As Reagan watches arm-wrestling videos on the computer, I leave the office and slip out the front door.

I lumber along the sidewalk with my head down. My brain is overloaded and my body feels weak. I'm way over my talk capacity. I've felt tired before, but nothing like this. With the sun setting behind me, I watch my shadow as I walk. My feet drag against the ground.

Then I hear a thud and pain shoots through my head. I drop to my knees, my vision hazy. Squinting, I hold one hand against my throbbing forehead and reach in front of me with the other. I feel a hard surface and when my vision finally clears, I see it's the side of a brick house. I kneel there for a moment, resting my body against the wall. I exhale, and then with one hand still pressed against my head, I get to my feet and begin to walk back home. I had left the house hoping to get rid of my headache, but now I'm returning with a bigger one.

***

The next morning I awake to see Reagan staring down at me.

"It's time for school," she says.

My head aches. "What time is it?"

"It's time to go," she says. "If you don't get up now, you're going to miss breakfast, and it's the third most important meal of the day."

"I thought it was the most important," I say, rubbing my eyes.

"It is important, it's just the third most," she says.

I lean up in bed. "But there are only three meals, so that would make it the least important."

"You need to get to bed earlier. Your brain's not working right."

I fall back into my bed, pulling the sheet over my head.

"Colin!" she screams through the sheets. "Let's go!"

At school, my head is still throbbing and my ears are ringing. It's a combination of talking-overload and the fact that I ran into a wall. Oh, and also because Reagan screamed in my face.

"What happened to your head?" Nate asks, as I cross through the cafeteria at lunch.

I smooth the bandage on my forehead. "I walked into a brick wall."

"You *literally* walked into a brick wall?" asks Nate.

"Yes."

"The chances of that happening are extremely slim," he says. "At least for someone who can see."

I set my lunch down.

"I'm almost done with my third book for the reading challenge," says Nate. "Are you close to finishing?"

"No."

"I thought we were going to stay in sync."

I blow out a breath of air. "Sorry, I haven't had time."

"But you've had time for the debate team."

"I know, but the debate's important. Nobody cares about the reading challenge."

Nate stares at me. "I care about it."

Perry reaches our table "Did an alien attack you?" he asks, noticing my bandage.

"He hit a brick wall," says Nate.

"Seriously?" says Perry.

"Yes!" I say. "I was walking and *literally* ran into a brick wall! Okay!"

"Sorry," says Perry. "I've just never heard of anyone doing that … you know because most people look straight ahead when they walk."

I feel my face flush. "Well I guess I'm just an idiot then!" I say, stomping away.

"Where are you going?" asks Perry.

I turn and scowl at him. "I'm going to a different table. Is that okay with you?"

"Yeah … I just thought you'd want to sit with your friends," says Perry.

"I don't want any friends right now," I say. "I just want to be left alone. Why doesn't anyone understand that?"

***

As students empty out of math the next day, I stay at my desk, staring into the hallway.

"Are you going to lunch?" Ms. Walsh asks.

"I don't know … I'm not really hungry."

She waits as the last student walks out. "Is everything okay, Colin?"

I rest my chin against the desk. "Yeah, I'm just tired."

"Is the debate taking a lot out of you?" she asks.

"That and my cousin."

Ms. Walsh stands from her desk and walks over. "Reagan, right?"

"Yeah. You know Reagan?"

"She's in one of my classes," she says, nodding.

My eyes widen. "I'm so sorry."

"You don't have to apologize," she says. "I like Reagan."

I look down. "You have to say that because you're her teacher."

"Maybe so," she says, shrugging, "but Reagan does have a lot to share."

"I know and she shares it all day long."

Ms. Walsh sits down in the desk next to me. "I imagine it's intimidating knowing that you'll have to debate her."

"Yeah." I glance around the empty classroom. "It's like you having to debate Mr. Melacki."

She laughs. "Yes, that would certainly be challenging."

"It would be impossible," I say.

"I'm not so sure about that," she says.

I sigh. "And there's so many people going now. What if I make a fool of myself?"

"Well, I think people are coming to support you," she says. "That's why I'm going."

Great. The faculty will be there, too.

She adjusts her glasses. "Can I give you some advice?"

"Sure," I say, lifting my head from the desk. "And sorry, I hope this doesn't make you tired. I know you're kind of quiet too."

"It might," she says. "But it's worth it."

"So what's your advice?" I ask.

"When it comes to the debate, don't worry about Reagan. Only worry about your argument."

"But I have to worry about Reagan. I need to out-talk her to win." I shake my head. "I don't think I can do it."

The corners of her lips curl up. "Just be yourself, Colin."

***

As I wait to board the bus home on Friday afternoon, I see Perry and Nate walking together. It's been two days since I've talked to them. I thought more time to myself would help, but for whatever reason, I feel worse.

Then I notice Ronald walk by, and as usual, he's looking down. He's wearing the same brown shirt and has it buttoned up to the collar.

"Hey, Ronald," I say.

He stops, keeping his head low, his eyes shifting back and forth as he scans the students.

I wave to him. "Right here, Ronald."

His face brightens when he sees me. "H—H—Hi, Colin."

"How's it going?" I ask.

"G—Good," he says. "You ride the bus?"

"Lucky number three-ten," I say.

Ronald glances at the bus. "Why's it lucky?"

"Well, I don't know how lucky it is now, but at one point I had sat by myself for forty-seven straight days."

"Really?" His eyes follow the long line of students waiting to board. "It looks like a full bus. W—What's your secret?"

Then I hear kids chuckling behind us. I peek over my shoulder and see the Botchaway brothers.

"What do you suppose the most challenging profession would be for a stutterer?" Larry asks Stanley.

Stanley faces his brother. "I would say a p—p—politian, for they do an awful lot of p—p—public speaking."

"How about a t—t—tv news anchor?" says Larry.

They're trying to keep their voices low, but I can hear them, and I can tell from the look on Ronald's face that he can hear them too.

"I think an a—a—auctioneer would be the most difficult," says Stanley. "Although you don't find many quiet auctioneers."

As I begin to say something, I see Ronald run off. "Ronald! Wait!"

I hurry after him, rushing along the line of buses, but Ronald doesn't look back. He crosses the street and turns onto the sidewalk. The crossing guard waves me through as I try to keep up.

"Ronald!"

He plows ahead, determined to get as far away from the school as possible. He continues down the sidewalk, walking hard, his head down. I break into a run. My backpack bounces against my back as I sprint past him on the grass.

I turn into his path, holding up my hand. "Stop!"

With his eyes still on the ground, Ronald crashes into me. We tumble into someone's front yard, Ronald falling over me.

Shifting onto my back, I feel a sharp pain in my shoulder. Ronald is on his side.

"Are you alright?" I ask.

He stares at me, his chest rising up and down.

I prop myself up on one arm. "It's okay," I say. "It's just me."

His breathing slows. I get to my feet, brush the dirt from my pants, and offer him my hand. He grabs it and I pull him up. His shirt is dirtier than ever and a leaf is caught in his hair.

"You have a leaf in your hair," I say.

He runs a hand along the right side of his head.

"The other side," I say, pointing.

Ronald pulls the leaf from above his left ear and lets it float to the ground. Then he sees a bus drive by. "I think you missed your bus."

"That's okay," I say, pressing a hand against my sore shoulder. "It's not too far of a walk."

"If you're hurt, I can ask my dad to drive you home." He points past me. "My house is right down the street."

"Thanks, but I'm okay. I can walk." I look back at the school. "It must be nice living so close."

"I couldn't handle riding the bus anyway."

"Why, because of boys like Larry and Stanley?"

He gives a weak nod.

"I'm sorry they made fun of your stuttering," I say.

His eyes narrow. "What? I don't care about that."

"You don't?"

"No," he says, shaking his head. "And it's almost gone now. I mean, d—do you care?"

"No, not at all." I laugh. "Your grammar's better than anyone I know."

He shrugs.

"So why did you run then?" I ask.

Ronald looks down. "Because they called me quiet. I know my stuttering will go away ... but I'll always be quiet." He pauses. "I know you're quiet too, Colin, but at least you don't care about it."

I swallow, hesitating for a moment. "I do care, Ronald."

His forehead crinkles. "No you don't ..."

My shoulders sag and I feel my stomach tighten. I stare at him blankly. "Yeah, I do," I say, my voice cracking. "I hate being called quiet. I hate it. I know I told you that I don't, but ... that was a lie." My eyes begin to water. "Sometimes I wish I wasn't quiet ... because I feel like there's something wrong with me. It's hard to explain. But it doesn't mean I don't like talking or I'm strange or anything." Tears run down my face and onto my shirt. "I know I can't talk as much as everyone else and I know I get tired easier, but I don't mind having a conversation with someone if I feel comfortable around them. I really don't." I clear my throat and blink hard as I realize something. "You know what, Ronald ... I don't think we're weird at all. It's just harder for us to open up to some people. That's it, that's all it is."

"But you're kind of opening up to me," he says.

"I know ... because I feel comfortable around you."

Ronald smiles. "Thanks, Colin."

I use my sleeve to dry the tears from my cheek.

"Do you want to eat lunch again sometime?" I ask.

"Sure, but ..."

"Don't worry, my table's all the way in the corner, away from the loud kids."

He shakes his head. "No, but what if I'm too tired to talk ... or don't have anything to say."

I consider what Ronald said, thinking back to Perry and Nate.

"Then just sit there," I say. "Because it stinks being alone. And if you ask me, it's better to sit there and be quiet, than not to sit there at all."

He nods and his crooked smile stretches farther across his face.

CHAPTER 8
THE DEBATE

That weekend, I leave messages with Perry and Nate, but neither calls me back. I ask Violet if she wants to try tennis again, suggesting a new court and promising that Reagan won't find us. Violet doesn't see how that's possible and declines, barricading herself in her room.

I call a few people from my soccer team, but everyone is away or busy. I even try to organize an extra practice session with Dexter and Todd. They both say they'll check their schedules and get back to me. I don't hear from either the rest of the weekend. I don't hear from anyone.

On Monday, I stay home from school, too depressed to get out of bed. What happened to my nice, quiet life?

Although my mother left fruit juice and crackers on my nightstand, I don't have much of an appetite. With the house empty, it would be a perfect time to catch up on my reading, but I don't feel like it.

In the afternoon, I move downstairs to the couch. I turn on the television and flip through the channels, not really paying attention to what's on.

Then I hear a knock at the door. I ignore it since it wouldn't be for me anyway.

KNOCK. KNOCK. KNOCK

"Go away," I say softly.

KNOCK. KNOCK. KNOCK. KNOCK.

I flip off the television, toss the remote down, and roll onto my back. "Nobody's here. Go away."

The chime of the doorbell echoes through the house. Then it rings again, over and over. Letting out a long sigh, I rise from the couch. I cross through the family room, open the door, and find Perry, Nate, Sophia, and Ronald standing outside.

"Hey, Colin," Perry says.

"What are you guys doing here?" I ask.

"We're here to help you," says Sophia.

I step onto the porch. "Help me with what?"

"Help you b—b—beat Reagan in the debate," says Ronald.

My eyes move to Nate. "Is that true?"

"Yes," says Nate.

"How do you guys know Ronald?" I ask.

"He came to our table at lunch," says Perry.

My eyes move between Perry and Nate. It feels like I haven't seen them in a month. "I know I've kind of been a pain lately. I'm sorry." I bite my bottom lip. "I do want friends ... a lot of friends … even if it makes me tired."

Perry puts a hand on my shoulder. "It's okay, Colin, we're all in this together."

"So do you think I can actually beat Reagan in a debate?" I ask them.

Ronald covers Nate's mouth. "D—D—Don't answer that, Nate."

***

After I set out some drinks and snacks, we all sit down at my kitchen table. Well, everybody except Perry, who's circling the table with his hands behind his back, whispering to himself.

"What could Colin do, what could Colin do …" Perry stops. "Will you know the topics ahead of time?"

I shake my head. "No, they tell us that day. And they only give us twenty minutes to prepare."

"That's going to make it challenging," says Perry. "The longer you have to prepare, the better your chances."

"Maybe Sophia can help," Nate says. "She's knows how to talk a lot."

"That's a good point," says Perry. "Sophia, any ideas?"

Sophia stares at me for a moment. "You need to practice."

That's her idea? To practice? I guess I shouldn't blame her though. She is a quarter quiet.

"I've been practicing with my debate team for weeks," I say. "I'm terrible."

"Don't practice debating," she says. "Practice talking."

"*Talking*?"

"Yeah," she says, nodding. "That's all debates are. Don't worry about the topic, just worry about talking as much as possible."

"Okay," I say.

"Why don't you try talking to me for as long as you can," she says.

"Sure." I turn my chair toward her and take a breath.

"Begin talking," Sophia says.

I stare at her. "Uh ... uh ... errr ..."

Perry tosses a few peanuts into his mouth. "I don't think it's working."

I drop my head. "Nothing's going to work ..."

"You just need a plan," Perry says. "Quiet kids work good with plans."

"Ms. Walsh said I should just be myself," I say.

Perry shakes his head. "Sorry, Colin, but that's not going to work with your personality. We need to get you talking up there."

"But I can't just become a talker. It doesn't work that way." I run my fingers through my hair. "It's like I need a burst."

"W—What do you mean?" says Ronald.

"When I was practicing with Reagan once, I got this burst of energy and I screamed something out. It was pretty good, but I couldn't sustain it."

Perry's eyes widen. "What if you could sustain it?"

"How?" I ask.

Perry leans against the wall and opens a soda. He stares at the can. "I have an idea."

"What?" asks Sophia.

"To have any chance of out-talking her, you're going to have to do three things." Perry says.

"Wait, wait, let me write this down." My hands shake as I grab a piece of paper and a pencil.

"First," Perry says, "you're going to have to stock up on your energy. Avoid talking as much as possible before Friday. Don't talk to anyone, not even your parents."

"That'll be hard, but I'll try."

"No, you can't *try*," Sophia says. "You have to do this if you want to win."

"Okay, okay …" I say.

"Second, you'll need to increase your energy level the night of the debate," says Perry. "Before and during dinner, drink as many sodas as possible, ten or twenty maybe."

"Twenty sodas? That seems like a lot."

Perry nods and pours more peanuts onto his hand. "You're right, that would make you sick and we can't have that. Maybe just three or four."

I scribble it down. "Three or four sodas, got it."

"And try to eat a lot of candy," he says.

I look up at him. "Why candy?"

"Because candy has a lot of sugar in it," he says. "It would be a good supplement to the sodas."

"Wow, okay," I say.

"Third, during the debate, don't get hung up on the topic. If something useful comes out about the topic, fine. If something else comes out, that's fine too. Remember what Sophia said. You just need to out-talk her."

I push out a breath and write it down.

Then Perry takes a swig of his soda. "And if none of that works, try giving her garlic."

"What would that do?" Sophia asks.

"Well, if she's not an alien, she might be a vampire."

"And garlic will destroy her?" I ask

"It just stuns them," says Nate.

"Yeah, but if you give her enough it might," says Perry. "Try fifty pounds."

"G—Garlic is usually measured in cloves," says Ronald.

***

On Tuesday, I return to my usual lunch table with Perry and Nate. Ronald joins us.

"Have you talked today?" asks Perry.

"No," I say.

Perry holds up his palms. "Seriously?"

"Sorry."

"You did it again," Perry says.

Perry grabs Nate's empty brown lunch bag and tears a section from it, making it into a sheet of paper. He slides it across the table to me.

"If you need to communicate, write it down," he says.

Ronald pulls a pen from his pocket. "Here's a p— pen."

I take it and begin writing. A few seconds later, I hand the brown sheet to Nate.

He reads it. "I'm sorry Perry tore your lunch bag. I know you like to recycle those."

Nate looks over at me. "It's okay, we can still recycle it."

Then I feel a hand on my back. Peeking over my shoulder, I see Dexter.

"How you doing, Colin?" he asks.

I lift my shoulders.

Dexter sits next to me. "Listen, I was thinking about adding an extra practice session this week. What do you think? Do you have time?"

Nate hands the brown sheet back to me and I begin writing again. A minute later, I give it to Dexter.

"I wrote this down because I can't speak to you," says Dexter, reading. "I'm trying to conserve my talking for the debate. Also, I'm sorry, but I won't be able to come to any practice sessions this week." Dexter squints, trying to follow my writing as it goes down the side of the sheet. "My friends came up with a plan that I really like and I think it gives me the best chance to win. I hope you understand."

"Well, I'd prefer if you worked with me and Todd since we're on the debate team," says Dexter. "Do any of your friends have debate experience?"

I give a confident nod.

"Not including the practice session with me?" says Dexter.

My lips turn down and I shake my head.

"Have any of your friends ever watched a debate?" asks Dexter.

I look to my friends.

"Yeah," they say.

"Not including the practice session with me?" says Dexter.

"No," they say.

"Will you reconsider, Colin?" asks Dexter.

I glance at Perry, Ronald, and Nate, thinking about it. Then I shake my head.

"Okay," says Dexter. "If you think their plan gives you the best chance to win, I'll support you." He flips over the brown sheet and finds something else, reading that as well. "Nate."

"Yes?" says Nate.

"No, your name is on this," says Dexter.

"It's my lunch bag," says Nate.

After Dexter walks off, the school intercom crackles and I hear Principle Reiland's voice. "Good afternoon, students. Just a reminder that debates one and two, between Kiss My Rebuttal and The Debate Team, will be held in the auditorium at 2:00pm on Friday afternoon. However, due to increased interest in the debate between Reagan Murphy and Colin Quigley, the third debate will be moved to 8:00pm."

Perry smiles wide. "They're moving you to prime time."

Reaching across the table, I grab the paper bag. I write something down, and then flip it around so Perry can see it.

He tilts his head, reading. "But Friday is pizza night."

***

To further build up my talk-capacity, I use every talk-reducing strategy I know of the rest of the week. I sit by myself on the bus, I pretend to have laryngitis for a day, I skip recess by faking a sprained ankle, and I rush through dinner to avoid any table conversation.

My parents ask if anything is wrong, but I just shake my head. And when they inquire as to why I hurry through dinner, I just point to my textbooks. It's an easy, nonverbal way of saying I have a lot of homework. I feel bad, but it's the only chance I have to beat Reagan.

On Friday afternoon, I watch Dexter debate Larry, and Todd debate Stanley. My team does well, winning four of the six topics. We need to win five to take the entire debate, so I'll only need to beat Reagan once.

At 7:45 p.m., I sneak into the parking lot and slam two sodas, which should get me going. I've also stashed three more sodas on the podium and my pockets are stuffed with Hershey's Chocolates.   After I finish my second soda, I glance around the parking lot. I've never seen it so crowded and cars continue to roll in. A line of them stretches from the school entrance to the intersection a half-mile down the street.

I spend the next fifteen minutes pacing backstage, rubbing my hands together. I'm raring to go. My talk-capacity, which is normally three-hundred and thirteen words, must be into the thousands.

Separating the curtains, I peek out at the audience. Every seat in the auditorium is taken. There are two main sections with an aisle down the center. The left side is filled with the loudest kids in school, along with Mr. Melacki and the other talkative teachers. I can feel the floor shake with all of their hooting and yelling.

The right side of the room is filled with the quiet students and teachers, including Ms. Walsh. They're being, well, quiet. They sit, looking straight ahead, with their hands on their laps.

Principle Reiland walks down the main aisle. He reaches a table in the front of the auditorium, sets down his coffee, and spreads out a few papers.

"Welcome students, faculty, and families of John Quincy Adams Middle School," Principle Reiland says. "We're glad to have you with us this evening for the third and final debate between Kiss My Rebuttal and The Debate Team. As I did with the first two debates, I'll explain the rules." He pauses. "Three judges, consisting of John Quincy Adams Middle School teachers, will be evaluating each debate based on these criteria." Principle Reiland looks down. "Quality of argument, delivery, time management, counter arguments, and overall impression." He turns to the audience. "We will now bring out our two debaters. From Kiss My Rebuttal, Reagan Murphy."

The left side of the audience erupts in applause as Reagan strides onto the stage. The kids yell and shout, their fists clenched, their arms in the air.

"And from The Debate Team, Colin Quigley."

I feel everyone's eyes on me as I slip out from behind the curtain. A few soft claps echo through the room as I walk to the podium. Then it goes silent. My hands are shaking and my eyes are shifting wildly from side to side. I'm ready to talk!

Reagan glances at me from the other podium. She's always ready to talk, so she doesn't look any different.

"Reagan and Colin, you will be asked to argue for or against a particular topic," Principle Reiland says. "There will be three topics given with fifteen minutes allotted for each. The judging panel will announce a winner after each topic is debated; however, we will use all nine debates, including the six from this afternoon, when determining the winning team." He pauses. "This is a SPAR-style debate and interruptions are allowed, but we ask that they be done in a courteous and professional manner. Once the topic has been read, you will have twenty minutes to prepare." He motions to the stacks of books and papers. "You are only permitted to use the materials located on the tables behind you. Once the twenty minute preparation period has ended, you'll be asked to return to your podiums and begin the debate." Principle Reiland takes a drink of his coffee and sits down. "Let us begin."

The audience cheers, although only the left side.

"Topic one," Principle Reiland says. "Video games offer more benefits than drawbacks. Colin, you will argue for. Reagan, you will argue against." He glances at the clock. "Your preparation time starts … *now*."

Reagan folds her arms. "I don't need any preparation time."

"You're forfeiting your preparation for this topic?" asks Principle Reiland.

"I don't need preparation for *any* of the topics," says Reagan.

The loud kids scream and holler.

"Silence please," says Principle Reiland, and then looks to me. "Colin, this doesn't affect you. You can still take your full twenty minutes."

I glance at Dexter and Todd. They both mouth 'yes.' Then my eyes move to Perry, Nate, Sophia, and Ronald, who are in the front row. They all nod.

Staring into the audience, I think about it. If I'm going to beat a talker, I need to act like a talker. A talker wouldn't prepare anything. A talker would just talk. I have to rely on my stored up talk-capacity, the pocketfuls of candy, and the sodas. If I have prepared as well as think I have, I should be able to open my mouth and the words will rush right out.

"I decline my preparation time as well," I say. "For all topics."

The crowd gasps and my team drops their heads.

"Then the debate shall start," says Principle Reiland. "Colin … please begin."

Having no idea what I'm about to say, I open my mouth. Something I remember reading about in a gaming magazine flies out.

"Video games are a multi-billion dollar business, and that means more jobs, including right here in Virginia." I grip the sides of the podium as my hands continue to shake. "Video games also support local real estate, lead to improvements in software development, and help kids develop strategic thinking." I point to Perry. "Like my friend Perry, who's going to use his video game experience to help defeat the aliens when they invade." Then I hold up a finger. "And let's not forget the most important reason—they're a lot of fun!"

"Just because video games add jobs to the economy doesn't mean they're beneficial for the kids playing

169

them," says Reagan. "Unless you consider moving your thumbs as exercise."

The students in the loud section laugh.

"That's not true," I say. "A lot of games use your entire body, which helps improve hand-eye coordination."

"But why would you need to improve your hand-eye coordination?" ask Reagan. "So you can play *more* video games."

The loud kids roar.

"Kids would be better off playing actual sports outside," Reagan continues.

"But that's the point of video games," I say. "They allow you to experience things you can't experience in the real world, like a one-hundred pin bowling alley."

"It's still not—" Reagan starts, but I cut her off.

"And that may lead to an actual one-hundred pin bowling alley. That's the other thing about video games—they inspire great ideas." I press both hands against the podium and my eyes grow large. "You know, I may just build one."

Reagan rolls her eyes. "You're going to build a one-hundred pin bowling alley?"

I give a sharp nod. "Yes!" I take a breath and sneak a drink of soda. "Now, a one-hundred pin bowling alley would cost more than a regular bowling alley because you would have to buy a lot more pins, but I'd have more customers because kids would rather knock down a hundred pins than ten. So everyone who would normally go to a regular bowling alley would come to my bowling alley—Colin's One Hundred Pin Bowling Alley.'"

"That's a stupid name," Reagan says.

My mind is processing thoughts at a frantic pace. I ignore Reagan and continue.

"But I'd have to special-order that contraption thing that picks up the pins because a regular one only picks up ten pins, not a hundred." I pause, thinking about it. "And the building would need to be a lot bigger than a regular bowling alley because the lanes would have to be large enough to fit a hundred pins. So if I wanted the same amount of lanes, the building would have to be ten times as big." I glance at Nate, who's staring at me with wide eyes. "Is that right, Nate? Ten times as big? No, never mind, you can't answer. And I know it's right."

Reagan tries to counter. "I don't think your idea has anything to do with—"

"I wonder if the balls would need to be bigger," I say, talking over her again. "Could a regular size bowling ball knock down a hundred pins? I'd have to test that."

Principle Reiland interjects. "Let's try to stay on topic."

"Thank you Principle Reiland, I agree," says Reagan. She looks over at me. "Colin, you said a moment ago that playing video games helps improve hand-eye coordination. Is that correct?"

"Yes."

"So you're suggesting that if someone were to play a lot of tennis video games, they would become a better tennis player. Correct?"

"Yeah."

"So why is it that *I*, who has never played a tennis video game, beat *you*, who's played like a million times, in an actual tennis match?'

I hear oohs and aahs from the audience.

"Uh …"

"And how many shots do you think you've taken in soccer video games," Reagan asks. "Probably thousands, right?"

"Yeah … so?"

"*So*, I let you shoot on me over twenty times using an actual soccer ball. But how many times did you score?"

I hesitate.

"*None,*" Reagan says. "And why is it that *I*, who has never played a sword dueling video game, beat *you*, who's played like a billion times, in an actual sword fight?"

"Well ..."

"The two of you had an actual sword fight?" asks Principle Reiland.

I notice my parents in the audience. They sink into their chairs, their mouths open.

"Yes," says Reagan. "And I destroyed him."

"Well I'm glad to see that you're both okay," Principle Reiland says. "Colin, do you have a counter."

My energy level is fading. "I ... I ..."

Principle Reiland holds up a hand. "Then let's stop there."

As the judges huddle, I take three gulps of soda and pop a few chocolates into my mouth.

Then Principle Reiland returns to his seat. "After consulting with the judges, the winner of topic one is ... *Reagan Murphy.*"

A thunderous applause echoes from the loud section. Larry and Stanley flash casual grins as if they were already expecting Reagan to win. Dexter and Todd clap, trying to encourage me. I need to win the next topic. I swallow down my chocolates and feel a surge.

"Let's move to topic number two," Principle Reiland says. He takes a drink from his coffee, and then reads. "The U.S. Postal Service should end mail delivery on Saturdays." His eyes turn up. "Reagan, you will start this time. You will argue for and Colin will argue against. And since neither debater will be taking preparation time … please begin."

Reagan straightens behind the podium. "Delivering mail on Saturday eats up a lot of extra gas. And it's all to deliver stupid love letters and video games that could have waited until Monday. Not to mention, if you did need something important delivered, like the *Legend of Joe Mufferaw* book, then you could have FedEx or that brown company deliver it for you."

"Your statements are contrada … flicting," I say. "You said it eats up a lot of gas to deliver mail on Saturday, but also said that if something important needs to be delivered, like a book on a lumberjack, then you could use UPS or that blue and red company to deliver it."

"So what?" says Reagan.

"Well they'd be using the same gas. So if the packages are being delivered anyway, why can't the

174

Postal Service do it? You gain absolutely nothing by ending Saturday delivery."

Reagan shakes her head. "But it wouldn't be the same amount of gas because it would only be the important packages being delivered, like lumberjack books. Stupid things, like your video games, could wait until Monday."

I peer over at her. "But what if it was a lumberjack video game that was being delivered?"

"They have lumberjack video games?" she asks, excited.

"Yes," I say.

She presses her lips together. I think I've stumped her.

"It doesn't matter," she says. "All video games are stupid, even lumberjack video games."

After going back and forth for another five minutes about what packages are considered important, my talk-capacity has dwindled again and my eyes feel heavy. I need to fight through it.

"And not only should they continue Saturday delivery," I say, "they should add Sunday as well."

A puzzled expression fills Principle Reiland's face.

"Why should they add Sunday?" asks Reagan.

"Because it would help with my schedule," I say.

Her brow furrows. "Your schedule?"

I nod. "Yes, because as part of my chores, I get the mail every day at 4:00pm. And it throws me off on Sunday when there's no mail. So if the Postal Service delivered mail every day, it would keep my schedule consistent, which would be good because I don't really know what to do during that three minute window every Sunday."

"Colin, postal workers need days off too," she says. "They're not going to work an extra day just so you won't feel weird for three minutes every Sunday."

I bet I'd be a good mailman. All that alone time in the mail truck would be so ...

Focus!

I finish the rest of my first soda, and then chug half of another.

"What about McDonalds?" I say. "They're open on Sundays. Why doesn't the Postal Service just do shifts like McDonalds? You could have one driver who works Monday through Thursday and another driver who works Friday through Sunday."

"Who would want to work Friday through Sunday?" Reagan asks.

"Someone who *doesn't* want to work Monday through Thursday. And just think how great it would be

176

to get video games delivered on Sundays." I look into the audience, finding my father. "Dad, can you drive me to the post office tomorrow? I want to put this idea in their suggestion box."

Reagan slams her fist against the podium. "They're not going to deliver mail on Sundays just because of your suggestion!"

I slam my fist down to match her. "Why not!"

"Because it's a terrible idea!"

No response comes to me. I shove five more pieces of chocolate into my mouth and another completely unrelated thought fills my brain. "Do you think horses care that we ride on top of them?" I look over at Dexter. His eyes are narrowed and his head is tilted. He looks like a confused dog. "It's got to be so annoying," I continue, "to have someone jump on your back whenever they feel like it. I know I wouldn't like it if a horse tried to jump on my back. It doesn't seem fair."

Reagan's eyes turn toward the ceiling. I don't think she can handle my wild, caffeine-induced thinking.

"What does this have to do with ending mail delivery on Saturday?" she asks.

"Nothing, but I think I'm going to start a petition to end horseback riding too" I say, and then look at my dad again. "Dad, after we stop by the post office to drop off my suggestion about Sunday mail delivery, can we go into town so I can start getting signatures for my anti-horseback riding petition?"

My dad glances around the audience, and then shrugs.

I spend the next two minutes making the same argument about camels and elephants, and then talk about whether I'll need a separate petition for each animal. Unfortunately this rambling has zapped my talk-capacity.

"That's time," says Principle Reiland. "And let's remember to stay on topic." He exhales, then takes a drink of coffee. I don't think he's had to moderate a debate like this.

My friends shift anxiously in their seats as Principle Reiland whispers with the judges. The same smug look remains on Larry and Stanley's faces.

Principle Reiland returns to his seat a minute later. "The winner of topic two," he says, "is *Reagan Murphy*."

The loud section erupts again, cheering and howling, and I can feel the auditorium shake. Dexter and Todd hang their heads. My team's lead is gone. If I lose the last topic, we lose the debate. But I need to forget about it. I need to remember Perry's advice and keep talking.

"This will be our third and final debate topic," Principle Reiland says. He looks down and reads. "Virginia should end its attempt to lure a professional sports team to our state. Colin, will argue for and Reagan will argue against." He takes a breath. "Please begin."

I suck down the rest of my second soda and feel another rush. "Virginia doesn't need a professional sports team and we shouldn't waste *my* hard earned tax dollars trying to get one."

"You don't work," says Reagan. "You're not contributing any taxes."

"My *dad's* hard earned tax dollars," I say, and then notice my mom in the audience. "Oh, I forgot about my mom. She works too, mostly in the garden."

"Please continue with your argument," Principle Reiland says with a sigh.

"Yes, so should we spend our money trying to convince a team of old, spoiled, overpaid athletes to come to Virginia? Or should we use that money to increase teachers' salaries?" I say, motioning to Principle Reiland and the other judges. "And for those who would like to see a professional football or baseball game, the Orioles, Nationals, Ravens, *and* Redskins all play within a few hours."

"And you think what *I* said was contradaflicting," Reagan says. "That was the most contradaflicting statement I've ever heard." She points at me. "You said we shouldn't spend our money on professional athletes in Virginia, but also suggested that we go watch these *same* athletes outside of our state."

"I didn't say—"

"That's money we could be spending *right here* in Virginia if we had a professional sports team," she says, jabbing her finger against the podium.

As I open another soda, Reagan continues. "And for each professional sports team, one billion dollars is put back into the local economy," she says. "And for each billion dollars, forty-two thousand extra jobs are created. So, as an example, Texas, which has eight professional sports teams, gets eight billion more dollars than Virginia, and that works out to six-hundred and fifty-one thousand extra jobs."

"Well first, there's no way Texas has eight sports teams," I say, and then belch.

"Count 'em, Colin," she says, using her huge fingers. "The Cowboys, Texans, Mavericks, Rockets, Spurs, Rangers, Astros, and Stars."

Wow, she's right. I can't believe Texas has eight professional sports teams.

"But there's no way Texas gets a billion dollars per team," I say.

She nods. "It is a billion. I read it on the Internet so I know it's right."

I shake my head. "But your math is wrong about how many jobs are created."

"It's right," she says.

"How do you know?" I ask.

"Because I'm awesome at math," she says, glaring over at me. "Teachers have told me that I'm better at math than Nate Dabrowski."

I hold her gaze. "Reagan, I *know* Nate Dabrowski. I've done math with Nate Dabrowski. Reagan Murphy, you are no Nate Dabrowski."

The quiet section claps and stomp their feet. No yelling though as their mouths remain closed.

"You may want to rethink your argument," Reagan says. "Because right now, Texas is beating you eight to nothing."

I squint at her. "Texas is beating us in what?"

"In how many sports teams we have."

"It's not a game. How can Texas beat us in sports teams?"

181

Reagan leans over the podium. "It is a game, and we're beating you eight to nothing."

I raise my shoulders. "Well our state was founded first."

"What?"

"Virginia was founded and made a colony in 1607. Texas was founded in like eighteen-something."

"Who cares?"

"We're beating you in being founded first."

"That's ridiculous."

I raise my hands. "First in being founded! Virginia's awesome!"

This is a ridiculous statement, and I realize that, but I need to stick to Perry's plan. I need to keep talking. It doesn't matter what gibberish happens to come out.

"Debaters," Principle Reiland says, his voice rising. "Let's stay on topic."

Reagan stares at me, shaking her head. "You're weird. You are not a good debater. The things you're saying are just *crazy*."

I think she's wearing down. I need to keep talking and go for the knockout.

"And who knows, we could end up having a team with a terrible name, like the Nationals. I mean what is a National? I thought it was a type of emergency." I shrug. "Maybe they did it on purpose." I wave my hands frantically. "Come quick, come quick, we're playing baseball! It's a Nationals emergency!"

Reagan shakes the podium, frustrated. "What are you talking about?"

I barely hear her as something else flies through my head. "My favorite sports team is the Vancouver Canucks. I don't know what a Canuck is, and I'm not even that crazy about hockey, but I love saying their name. *Ca—nuck. Ca—nuck. Ca—nuck.*"

Principle Reiland taps his hand against the table. "Topic, please …"

I can't stop. My head is filled with favorites and they all have to come out. This must be how a loud person feels. I talk for three minutes about my favorite sports, my favorite conferences within my favorites sports, my favorite divisions within my favorite conferences, and my favorite teams within my favorite divisions.

"Stop!" Reagan says. "Favorites is not the topic! Why won't you stop talking?" She shakes her head. "What are you going to tell us next? Your favorite color?"

"It's brown," I say. "It used to be blue, but I switched it." I finish my soda and keep talking. "My favorite bird is an Oriole, although strangely enough my favorite baseball team isn't the Baltimore Orioles, it's the Oakland Athletics. Although, as I mentioned, the Orioles are my favorite team within the American League East, which is my favorite division."

Principle Reiland stands, waiving his hand. "Topic, please, topic please …"

"And did you know that my favorite plates aren't round," I say. "They're square."

Reagan squeezes her eyes shut. "*What*?"

"I prefer the square plates because I don't like my food to touch." I grimace, thinking about my pork chops touching my corn. "It's easier to separate everything when you have four corners."

Reagan screams into the microphone. "Please stop talking!"

I struggle to keep my eyes open. I don't think the soda is helping because I'm starting to crash. "My uh ... my favorite animal is ... is a beaver."

"A beaver?" says Reagan. "Come on ..."

"What's wrong with that? I like beavers. I think it's really cool that they can chew through wood." I slip my last three chocolates into my mouth. "And speaking of wood, I like pine the best. Oak and maple are okay, but nothing beats a good piece of pine."

Reagan rubs her eyes. "A piece of what ... you're talking about *wood*? This is a debate about ... I don't even remember."

"Well, specifically pine. I just like the way it sounds—not as much as Canucks, but it's very soothing when you say it. *Pine. Pine. Pine ...*"

The chocolate didn't work. Everything goes dark and my head begins to drop.

"Oh my goodness," I hear Reagan say. "You're a complete nut. I can't do it ... I can't listen to this anymore."

"Reagan, can you please clarify your statement," Principle Reiland says.

"I'm done ..." she says

Principle Reiland presses his hands against the table, leaning forward. "What does that mean?" he asks. "Are you conceding?"

I lift my head and crack my right eye open, staring over at her.

"Reagan, are you conceding this debate?" Principle Reiland asks again.

There's a rumble through the audience, kids standing in shock. Well, at least kids from the loud section. The quiet kids remain seated, their mouths hanging open.

Reagan keeps her head down for a long moment.

Then she straightens her shoulders and blows out a breath. "No." She shakes her head. "Never. I'll talk all night if I have to."

The loud section cheers.

I slump over the podium and sigh. That was my only hope. I've lost the third round for sure, and with that, I've lost the debate. What was I thinking? How could I ever beat Reagan in a debate?

"Colin?" Principle Reiland says.

"I can't out-talk her," I say, my weak voice echoing through the auditorium. "No matter what I say or what I drink or how much candy I eat … I'll never be able to do it. A quiet kid can't out-talk a loud kid. It's impossible." I stare into the crowd and the somber faces of the quiet kids stare back. "I'm sorry."

"It's okay, Colin," Principle Reiland says. "You've done well."

I hear a few claps.

"You do have a minute left," Principle Reiland says, "but I assume you have nothing more to add for this topic?"

My eyes settle on Ms. Walsh. I know what she would say. *Just be yourself.* Well, I was … and I lost.

Principle Reiland says, "Very well. This is debate is—"

"Wait," I say, blinking hard. "But I wasn't myself."

"Excuse me," Principle Reiland says.

"You know what, I don't have to out-talk Reagan to win the debate," I say. "I have to out-debate her."

The quiet kids edge up in their seats.

"If there's one thing I've learned about debating, it's this," I say. "It's not the number of words you use that's important ... but the quality of those words. And if anyone can give a concise, well thought out argument, it's a quiet kid."

A smile spreads across Ms. Walsh's face.

I grip the podium. "If you ask me why I think Virginia should end its attempt to lure a professional sports team," I say, "I'll tell you exactly why. Because of everyone in this auditorium." I clear my throat. "It comes down to how Virginia should spend its time and money. Should we spend it on one team, whose players aren't even from Virginia? Or should we spend it on lots of teams—*local* teams, whose players live and go to school right here?" I say, tapping my finger. "Do we want to spend our time and money on one massive field that only a few players are allowed to play on? Or should we spend it on lots of fields that *everyone* can

play on?" I pause. "I love playing soccer at the park …
and I love watching football games at the high school.
And it's because I play on those fields and I know those
players. This state is great because of our
communities—because of everyone sitting in here." I
glance at my friends. "There's no need to lure any team
to Virginia. We already have everything we need."

The quiet section stands and claps. The ovation lasts
for a full minute.

"Quiet please," says Principle Reiland. "Reagan, do
you have a counter?"

She glances over at me and I see a surprised look on
her face. I don't think she was expecting that argument.

"Reagan?" Principle Reiland says.

"Yeah," she says. "Well … the …" Reagan
hesitates, trying to find the words.

The room is silent.

"Reagan?" Principle Reiland says again. "I need a
counter."

She opens her mouth, but doesn't say anything.

Principle Reiland checks his watch. "Sorry, that's
time."

The Botchaway brothers sink into their seats. A low
whisper fills the auditorium as the judges confer. I

exhale, still weary. My legs wobble and I shift them to balance myself.

A moment later, Principle Reiland makes an announcement. "I've spoken with our judges and the decision is unanimous."

Dexter and Todd lean forward.

"With a victory in the final debate," Principle Reiland says, "the winner of this year's John Quincy Adams Middle School debate is … Colin Quigley and The Debate Team."

The quiet section erupts into applause. They're yelling and screaming and whistling and hollering. I've never heard quiet kids this loud. Then I see Mr. Melacki walk from the loud section over to Ms. Walsh. He offers his hand and she shakes it. Then the loud kids and quiet kids move toward each other, shaking hands, patting backs, and hugging.

A few minutes later, there are no loud and quiet sections. Everyone is mixed together, talking. As I stagger away from the podium, my friends rush the stage and surround me. Principle Reiland cuts through them, a microphone in his hand.

"Colin, is there anything you'd like to say?" he asks, shouting over the crowd.

With Dexter and Todd supporting me, and my eyes half-open, I speak into the microphone with a raspy voice. "I just want to say one thing to my sister watching on the Internet stream back home. Yo, Violet, I did it!"

Then I collapse into my friend's arms.

CHAPTER 9

THE RECOVERY

I sleep for eighteen hours. When I finally wake up on Saturday, I'm too weak to get out of bed. My head is groggy and I feel like I've been hit by a dump truck.

There's a knock at my door and my mom peeks her head inside. "Hey ... you're awake."

I give a slight nod.

She steps over to my bed and places her palm against my forehead. "How are you feeling?"

"I ... I ..."

"It's okay, it's okay, don't talk." She pats me on my shoulder, a knowing look in her eyes. "I think I know what happened to you."

"What ..."

"Shhh," she says, covering my mouth. "You drank a lot of sodas before the debate, and now you're sick. Right? I saw a few cans missing from the fridge."

I nod, although that's only half the story.

"That's what I thought," she says. "I don't think you're ready for sodas just yet. Maybe when you start high school."

I wouldn't argue even if I had the energy. Sodas are bad news. They may give you a nice lift, but then it's crash city.

"I want you to stay in bed the rest of the day," she says. "Stay quiet and drink lots of water. Okay?"

I give a weak smile.

My mother squeezes my hand. "And congratulations on winning the debate last night. Your father and I were a little confused at parts, but we're very, very proud of you. I hope you know that." She looks down. "But I do have some sad news." My mother glances into the hallway, then back to me. "Reagan is a little homesick, so … she's going back to Texas."

I frown, hoping to appear as sad as possible. Although I am impressed that Reagan has honored our bet.

"Oh, and you have a visitor," she says. "Are you up for it?"

I nod.

My mother walks back to the door, whispers something to someone, and then Perry comes inside.

"Five minutes, Perry, that's it," my mother says. "And no talking, Colin."

Perry slides my desk chair over and sits down, facing me. "How you feeling, buddy?"

I shake my head and frown.

"That bad ... wow. Well, you did talk a lot."

My eyes widen and I nod.

"I still can't believe you beat Reagan in a debate," says Perry.

My lips curl into a smile. Perry stares at me with a gleam in his eyes. "It was the sodas, wasn't it? They got you through it."

I shrug.

Perry grins. "Yeah it was. I told you they were good."

I lean up in bed. "Listen, Perry."

"Colin, stop. Your mom said—"

"No, no, I want to say this." I take a breath. "I think you should stop drinking."

"What?"

"You should stop drinking sodas."

He drops his shoulders. "Why? I like sodas."

"I know, but ... you're not the same person when you drink."

"Come on, Colin, it's not a big deal."

"Please, Perry. Will you just think about it?"

Perry sighs and his eyes fall to the ground. I can see him thinking as his long fingers tap against the side of the chair. "Okay. If it means that much to you, I'll try and cut back."

My mom steps inside. "Alright, that's enough. Colin needs to rest."

Perry stands. "Sure, Mrs. Quigley." He reaches into his pocket and hands me something. "Nate wanted me to give this to you. It's a gift certificate, good for a free book at the bookstore."

"But he got this for the reading challenge," I say. "I never finished my three books."

"I think it's Nate's way of saying congratulations," he says.

"Come on, Perry," my mother says.

Perry heads for the door. After a few steps, he turns back, a proud smile on his face. "Thanks for winning one for us, Colin."

***

I'm still in a haze on Sunday. I hear Reagan is flying back in the evening, but I'm too worn out to celebrate. The debate has taken an enormous toll on my body. If I had uttered a few more words on Friday night, I might have ended up in the hospital. It's going to take several days to restore my talk-capacity.

As I sit up in bed and my vision begins to clear, I see Violet leaning against the doorframe.

"How long have you been standing there?" I ask.

She shrugs.

"Have you been waiting for me to wake up?"

Violet nods, walks to my bed, and then leans down and hugs me. "Thank you for getting her to leave."

She walks out without saying another word.

Sophia, Nate, and Ronald all call to see how I'm feeling. They insist that I don't talk though, and I appreciate it. I'm exhausted and I'll need more time before I can engage in a conversation. They understand that as long as I get time to myself, I'll be able to recharge and talk to them about the debate. Well, as long as it doesn't take more than three hundred and thirteen words.

Later that afternoon, my mom encourages me to go outside. She says a little walking will help with my recovery. Wearing my slippers and bathrobe, I step out the back door. I stroll around the yard, letting the sun warm my face. As I move along the fence, I see Larry and Stanley Botchaway in their backyard, adjusting a telescope.

"Master Quigley," Larry says, noticing me. "We're looking for radioactive jelly beans. Would you care to join us?"

I ignore them and keep walking. I circle the yard again and when I pass them a second time I'm surprised to hear their conversation.

"Let's try the sun," Stanley says.

"Yes," says Larry. "Father said it was a ten thousand dollar telescope. I imagine we could see sunspots."

I roll my eyes as I pass them. As smart as they are, the Botchaway brothers are going to blind themselves if they look at the sun through a telescope. I guess there are some things you can't learn from *The Great Gatsby*.

But there's no way, in my state, that I'm going to waste words on Larry and Stanley Botchaway. After a few more steps though, I stop and clear my throat, which is still sore from last night. "Don't look at the sun."

"I beg your pardon?" Larry asks.

"I said don't look at the sun through your telescope. It will ruin your eyes."

"Is that so?" Stanley says. He looks me up and down. "Why are you dressed like that?"

"I'm sick."

"What's wrong with you?"

"I talked too much."

Larry shakes his head at me. "You are a weird one."

I clench my fists. "Stop calling me weird!" I say through gritted teeth. "I am *not* weird! I'm just quiet! That's it!

They stare at me.

"And I'm telling you," I say, "if you look at the sun through your telescope, it will destroy your retinas."

Stanley raises an eyebrow. "I'm impressed you know what a retina is."

"I do. It's the back of your eyeball and if you damage it, you'll go blind."

"Well look at you, Master Quigley," says Larry.

"And by the way, you're not using 'Master' correctly. When you address a boy, you're suppose to use it before his first name."

Stanley smirks. "Perhaps you're a worthy intellectual adversary after all?"

"Uh … what's an adversary?" I ask. "Is that the same thing as a foe?"

"I believe that answers the question, now doesn't it," Stanley says.

"Hey," I hear a squeaky voice say.

I turn and see Reagan. Her eyes are droopy and her arms are resting against her side. "I'm leaving in an hour."

"Oh ... okay."

"So it should be quieter for you now. Just the way you like it."

I stare back, too exhausted to respond.

Reagan exhales. "You should try talking once in a while, Colin. You might just learn something."

She storms back into the house.

"Your cousin's leaving?" asks Larry.

"Yes," I say, my back still to him.

"Oh what a pity," Larry says. "If it wasn't for her, we would have won the debate."

I turn and face him, pointing a finger. "You know, the only reason I knew about the retina is because she told me. So if it wasn't for *her* you'd be blind right now."

As I stand there, I flash back to the conversation we had about the sun. I remember looking up what Reagan said because I didn't believe her. Unlike a lot of what she says, this turned out to be right. But what I remember most about the conversation was how confident she was in what she said. I could have never done that. I have to be a hundred percent certain about something before I'll talk about it.

Reagan may not always be right, but at least she's not afraid to put it out there. Although I may not have learned many facts from her, I did learn something. It takes guts to say something you're not sure about.

I'd like to tell her, but there's somewhere I need to go first. I find my mom and convince her to take me.

***

I see my dad backing out of the driveway as my mom turns back onto our street. "Mom, hurry," I say.

She honks her horn and comes to a quick stop in front of our house.

"Dad, wait!" I say, pushing the car door open.

I tear down the sidewalk, my jacket flapping behind me. My dad stops when he sees me.

As I reach his car, Reagan rolls down her window a few inches. I gaze down at her.

"What?" she asks.

I bend over, out of breath. "I … I liked your idea about the bite-sized tacos."

"Really?"

"Yeah. You know, it would be kind of cool to say 'I ate fifty tacos.'"

She rolls down her window the rest of the way. "And your idea about little pizzas as a topping wasn't bad either."

"Yes it was ... but thanks." My breathing begins to slow. "You don't have to leave if you don't want to."

"But I thought you liked it quiet."

"I do, but ... it was nice hanging out with you too." I look down. "I like being around someone who says what they think."

"Thanks, but I'm not sure everything I say is right."

"At least you're not afraid to say it."

She shrugs "Yeah … and I guess I am right like ninety-eight percent of the time."

"I think it's more like twelve percent."

She pokes me with her finger, and I look up.

"Do you mean that?" she asks.

"I … I wasn't trying to be mean."

"No," she says. "Do you mean that you want me to stay?"

I nod.

She grins. "Well, I kind of am."

"Really?" I ask. "I thought my dad was taking you to the airport."

"He is … but just to pick up my parents," she says. "We sold our house. We're going to start looking for a place up here now."

I glance at my house. "Are you going to stay with us while you look?"

"No. A hotel."

"Your family can stay here if you want."

She shakes her head. "My dad thought it would be a little cramped. Plus, it didn't seem right. You won the bet fair and square."

"It was just a dumb bet."

"Your house doesn't echo that well either." She peeks at my father, then looks back at me, keeping her voice low. "I know I can be a little loud sometimes. It's probably why I have trouble remembering things—because I spend too much time talking. I'll try to do more listening the next time I see you." She pauses. "And I'm sorry I called you weird. You're not."

I feel my body, which has been tense for the past few months, finally relax.

"Oh," I say, reaching into my coat pocket, "I got you something."

I pull out a book and hand it to her.

She takes it and stares at the cover. "*The Legend of Joe Mufferaw.*"

"Yeah."

"This is a ninety dollar book," she says.

"You can thank Nate," I say. "I used his gift certificate."

Reagan moves her hand over the cover. "You have some nice friends."

I nod.

Her eyes stay on the book. "I don't know what to say." She pauses for a long moment. "Thanks, Colin."

I smile, extending my hand to her.

She grabs it and shakes. The pain is excruciating, but I don't say anything. Reagan lets go, and then my dad backs the car onto the street. She pokes her head out of the window as they pull away. "You're okay, Quigley. You may be quiet, but you're scrappy. I like that!"

That's two-hundred and eighty-seven. But who's counting?

The End

About the Author

J.F. Wiegand is a software developer and author of the book, *Race to the Edge of the World*. He lives in Mount Airy, MD with his wife and three children.

Oh, and he's quiet.

If you enjoyed this book, please consider writing a review. You can find more about J.F. Wiegand at www.jfwiegand.com

63830676R00123

Made in the USA
Middletown, DE
05 February 2018